PLOT TO
CONTROL
THE WORLD

PLOT TO CONTROL THE WORLD

How the US Spent Billions to Change the Outcome of Elections Around the World

DAN KOVALIK

HOT BOOKS

Hot Books may be purchased in bulk at special discounts for sales promotion, corporate gifts, fund-raising, or educational purposes. Special editions can also be created to specifications. For details, contact the Special Sales Department, Skyhorse Publishing, 307 West 36th Street, 11th Floor, New York, NY 10018 or info@skyhorsepublishing.com.

Hot Books® and Skyhorse Publishing® are registered trademarks of Skyhorse Publishing, Inc.®, a Delaware corporation.

Visit our website at www.skyhorsepublishing.com.

10 9 8 7 6 5 4 3 2 1

Library of Congress Cataloging-in-Publication Data is available on file.

Cover design by Brian Peterson
Cover photo credit AP Images

ISBN: 978-1-5107-4500-1
Ebook ISBN: 978-1-5107-4501-8

Printed in the United States of America

CONTENTS

INTRODUCTION

As I WRITE THIS BOOK, THERE continues to be a panic in the halls of Washington and in newsrooms across the country about alleged Russian interference in US elections. So far, the sum total of the allegations, which will most likely never be tried or tested in court, is that (1) agents on behalf of Russia used social media, including Facebook and Twitter, to sew discord about already highly charged social issues—e.g., police violence, kneeling of NFL players during the playing of the National Anthem, and whether to continue publicly displaying confederate symbols and statues; and that (2) agents of Russia hacked into the computers of DNC officials and then proceeded to share correspondence through Wikileaks which revealed (quite truthfully) the DNC dirty dealings against Bernie Sanders during his 2016 presidential bid.

These allegations, and that is all they are at the present, have had a significant impact on free speech rights in the US. For example, President Trump has issued an Executive Order, quite broadly written, which would sanction foreign persons and entities, along with their US "agents" or investors, for engaging in a large spectrum of conduct, including what is determined to be the spreading of "propaganda" or "disinformation," if it is "undertaken with the purpose or effect of influencing, undermining confidence in, or altering the result or reported result of, the election, or undermining public confidence in election processes or institutions."[1]

In addition, both Facebook and Twitter, in response to claims that they did not do enough to prevent the alleged Russian interference into the 2016 elections, have begun to ban the accounts of over nine hundred people and groups they believe are misleading the public.[2] Such accounts that have been suspended, either temporarily or permanently, include those of right-wing conspiracy theorist Alex Jones and his Infowars show; the Venezuelan-funded news outlet, Telesur English; the American Herald Tribune; and a number of Iranian and Russian news outlets.

In the interest of full disclosure, I myself appeared on Infowars once, have written for and appeared on Telesur English, have written for the American Herald Tribune, and am often interviewed by Iranian and Russian news outlets, such as Press TV and RT. Quite possibly my Facebook and/or Twitter accounts will be banned, and quite possibly I, who am very critical of the US and its functioning as a democracy, will be sanctioned under the above-cited Executive Order as an alleged "agent" of some of these outlets for the purpose of purveying information which somehow "undermin[es] public confidence . . . in election processes or institutions." Maybe this book will even be the catalyst for such charges.

In any case, another account banned by Facebook is that of Cambridge Analytica, a UK-based firm which has become notorious as of late for collecting behavior data on over two hundred million Americans—data which the Trump Campaign used to advance his 2016 presidential campaign.[3]

A pertinent fact about Cambridge Analytica is that the US State Department also contracted with that firm after 2017 in order to "to influence elections in dozens of countries around the world."[4] But of course, this should not be surprising, for the US has been meddling and interfering in other countries' elections and democratic processes for years. And it has done so in quite ruthless and brutal ways which make the alleged Russian interference in the 2016 elections look like mere child's play.

As the *New York Times* quite rightly explained in February of 2018:[5]

> Bags of cash delivered to a Rome hotel for favored Italian candidates. Scandalous stories leaked to foreign newspapers to swing an election in Nicaragua. Millions of pamphlets, posters and stickers printed to defeat an incumbent in Serbia.
>
> The long arm of Vladimir Putin? No, just a small sample of the United States' history of intervention in foreign elections.
>
> . . .
>
> Most Americans are understandably shocked by what they view as an unprecedented attack on our political system [by Russia]. But intelligence veterans, and scholars who have studied covert operations, have a different, and quite revealing, view.
>
> "If you ask an intelligence officer, did the Russians break the rules or do something bizarre, the answer is no, not at all," said Steven L. Hall, who retired in 2015 after 30 years at the C.I.A., where he was the chief of Russian operations. The United States "absolutely" has carried out such election influence operations historically, he said, "and I hope we keep doing it."

These interventions, the *NYT* explains, while spearheaded by the CIA for the first several decades, are now largely instigated by the US State Department and the National Endowment for Democracy (NED), which was founded by President Ronald Reagan in the 1980s.

The *NYT*, citing an academic study published in Oxford University's *International Studies Quarterly*, relates that the US

PLOT TO CONTROL THE WORLD

admittedly meddled in foreign elections on at least eighty-one occasions between 1946 and 2000.[6]

This list of eighty-one cases of US election meddling *per se* is certainly not exhaustive, even up to the year 2000, and does not even purport to include the even more serious instances of US-backed coups and assassinations which actually destroyed democratic institutions in foreign lands. As historian and author William Blum summarizes:

> The secret to understanding US foreign policy is that there is no secret. Principally, one must come to the realization that the United States strives to dominate the world. . . . To express this striving for dominance numerically, one can consider that since the end of World War Two the United States has:
>
> - Endeavored to overthrow more than 50 foreign governments, most of which were democratically-elected.
> - Grossly interfered in democratic elections in at least 30 countries.
> - Waged war/military action, either directly or in conjunction with a proxy army, in some 30 countries.
> - Attempted to assassinate more than 50 foreign leaders.
> - Dropped bombs on the people of some 30 countries.
> - Suppressed dozens of populist/nationalist movements in every corner of the world.

Meanwhile, our nation's paper of record could not allow its acknowledgment of serial US interference to detract from the paper's eternal mission to promote American Exceptionalism—that is, the idea that the US is a unique force for democracy and freedom in the world. Thus, the *NYT* goes on to argue that, "in recent decades, . . . Russian and American interferences in elections have not been morally equivalent. American interventions have generally been aimed at helping non-authoritarian candidates challenge dictators or otherwise promoting democracy. Russia has more often intervened to disrupt democracy or promote authoritarian rule . . . ."

The *NYT* makes this claim without any supporting evidence, and indeed despite the fact that in the immediately preceding paragraph, it explained that "[t]he United States' departure from democratic ideals sometimes went much further [that mere propaganda campaigns]. The C.I.A. helped overthrow elected leaders in Iran and Guatemala in the 1950s and backed violent coups in several other countries in the 1960s. It plotted assassinations and supported brutal anti-Communist governments in Latin America, Africa and Asia."

A very abbreviated list of anti-democratic coups and brutal regimes the US helped to give birth to include the death squad regimes in El Salvador and Guatemala (supported by the US into the 1990s); the Colombian paramilitary state (supported until the present time); Iraq's Saddam Hussein dictatorship (backed until 1990); the dictator Mobutu Sese Seko in Zaire (supported into the early 1990s); the 2002 coup against democratically elected Venezuelan President Hugo Chavez; and the right-wing coup governments in Honduras and Ukraine (both backed until the present time).

All of these instances of foreign interference certainly took place in "recent decades," unless, of course, that term has no meaning at all. But the *New York Times*, of course, simply pretends otherwise. It further ignores the fact that somehow, and seemingly inexplicably, the US currently gives military support to 73 percent of the world's dictatorships.[7] Thus, rather than being an exception, or a "departure from democratic ideals" as the *New York Times* puts it, the US's intervention in other countries in the interest of promoting dictatorship is in fact the rule.

This type of sleight of hand, performed here by the *New York*

Times in the course of one short article, was eloquently explained by Harold Pinter, in his 2005 Nobel Prize acceptance speech. Pinter explains not only the fact that of the US's cruel foreign interventions, but also how the US has been uniquely adept at being able to convince the world, despite all evidence to the contrary, of its inherent goodness:

> The United States supported and in many cases engendered every right wing military dictatorship in the world after the end of the Second World War. I refer to Indonesia, Greece, Uruguay, Brazil, Paraguay, Haiti, Turkey, the Philippines, Guatemala, El Salvador, and, of course, Chile. The horror the United States inflicted upon Chile in 1973 can never be purged and can never be forgiven.
>
> Hundreds of thousands of deaths took place throughout these countries. Did they take place? And are they in all cases attributable to US foreign policy? The answer is yes they did take place and they are attributable to American foreign policy. But you wouldn't know it.
>
> It never happened. Nothing ever happened. Even while it was happening it wasn't happening. It didn't matter. It was of no interest. The crimes of the United States have been systematic, constant, vicious, remorseless, but very few people have actually talked about them. You have to hand it to America. It has exercised a quite clinical manipulation of power worldwide while masquerading as a force for universal good. It's a brilliant, even witty, highly successful act of hypnosis.[8]

Let us then briefly awaken from this hypnotic state and take a look at a number of the emblematic cases of US interference in other countries which, by design, had catastrophic results for the people and their pursuit of democracy and freedom.

1

THE FOREIGN POLICY OF THE UNITED STATES IS INTERVENTION

AS I WRITE THIS BOOK, IT has just been revealed that President Trump met on several occasions with dissident Venezuelan military officers to discuss plans for a coup against democratically elected President Nicolas Maduro. According to the *New York Times*, again pretending that such intrigue is largely a thing of the past, "[e]stablishing a clandestine channel with coup plotters in Venezuela was a big gamble for Washington, given its long history of covert intervention across Latin America. Many in the region still deeply resent the United States for backing previous rebellions, coups and plots in countries like Cuba, Nicaragua, Brazil and Chile, and for turning a blind eye to the abuses military regimes committed during the Cold War."[9]

Of course, this was not the first time in recent years the US was involved in supporting a coup in Venezuela. Thus, in 2002, the US, through the monetary assistance of the NED and United States Agency for International Development (USAID), the detailed foreknowledge of the CIA, and the encouragement of senior White House officials, helped to lay the groundwork for the coup against President Hugo Chavez in which he was forcibly led away by rogue military forces and flown to a remote island on Good Friday.[10] The US was also one of the few countries that quickly and unequivocally recognized the coup government, which wasted no time in declaring void the popularly created Constitution, firing the Attorney General, and dismissing the Supreme Court and democratically elected National Assembly.[11] While the coup was short-lived, with the people rising up to return Chavez to power on Easter Sunday, the US had shown its true colors, and its utter disdain for the democratic processes of another sovereign country.

In thinking about particular instances of US foreign meddling, intervention, and invasion, it is critical to realize that none of these instances were somehow aberrations. Rather, they have been, and continue to be, part and parcel of a consistent, seamless, and unwavering policy of the United States dating back to colonial times, and they are firmly supported by an ideological belief system which rises to the level of a religious faith.

This faith has a name, and it is Manifest Destiny—the belief that the expansion of the United States from the Atlantic to the Pacific of North America, and beyond, was and is not only inevitable, but is in fact a God-given moral right.[12]

Put in more crass terms, this is the notion that, as white, Christian, and freedom-loving people, we are uniquely good, and therefore have the unique right to expand throughout the world and intervene where we please without limitation. Indeed, any resistance put up to our expansion and intervention is unacceptable, immoral, and punishable by extreme violence. This part of the faith was explicitly set forth in 1845 by the person who coined the term "Manifest Destiny," John L. O'Sullivan, then-editor of the Democratic Party newspaper, who condemned England and France "'for the avowed object of thwarting our policy and hampering our power, limiting our greatness and checking the fulfillment of our manifest destiny to overspread the continent allotted by Providence for the free development of our yearly multiplying millions.'"[13]

A key tenet of this faith holds that we are uniquely good, and therefore privileged to do as we wish anywhere in the world, even when we do uniquely bad and horrible things to other peoples in the process of our international endeavors. It is not our actions and their effects which should be looked at, the faith provides, or even the *specific* intentions motivating particular actions. Rather, it is our inherent and profound goodness, and our *general* desire to do good, which matter and which justify our expansion and foreign interloping.

And so, the fact that US expansion in North America was carried out through the mass removal, plunder, rape, and physical elimination of millions of Native Americans and Mexicans occupying the land which God gave us, and through the oppression of hundreds of thousands of Africans brought over as slaves to build our country, in no way takes away from the goodness of us as a nation or a people, or from the rightness of our expansion project.

As the Encyclopedia Britannica explains, "the idea of Manifest Destiny was used to validate continental acquisitions in the Oregon Country, Texas, New Mexico, and California. The purchase of Alaska after the Civil War briefly revived the concept of Manifest Destiny, but it most evidently became a renewed force in US foreign policy in the 1890s, when the country went to war with Spain, annexed Hawaii, and laid plans for an isthmian canal across Central America."[14]

And, while the words "Manifest Destiny" have rarely been uttered in decades—most likely due to sheer embarrassment with the obviously Messianic notions these words evoke—the belief system represented by these words continues unabated to justify US intervention and aggression to this day. Indeed, as the devil himself, this doctrine goes by many names, such as American Exceptionalism.

Those who have experienced the wrath of this religion, on the other hand, call it by names such as Colonialism, or neo-Colonialism, or Imperialism. However, such words are simply verboten when speaking about the United States.

Indeed, Jeane Kirkpatrick, who would soon become UN Ambassador under President Reagan, stated as much in 1979, explaining in what would become a famous and quite influential piece in *Commentary* magazine: "[i]f, moreover, revolutionary leaders describe the United States as the scourge of the 20th century, the enemy of freedom-loving people, the perpetrator of imperialism, racism, colonialism, genocide, war, then they are not authentic democrats or, to put it mildly, friends. Groups which define themselves as enemies should be treated as enemies."[15] In short, if you use the "C" word or the "I" word in talking about the US, you are an enemy, plain and simple.

Imperialism especially is a word which dare not speaketh its own name. One of the few American intellectuals who was willing to utter this term, however, was Mark Twain who indeed helped to found the Anti-Imperialist League.

Mark Twain was one of the first great Americans to see the rottenness and hypocrisy of the American faith in unbridled expansion, and the dire consequences of pursuing it, and he called it out in only the way he could. Thus, Twain wrote the following piece in 1906 upon hearing of one of the more legendary massacres, "The Moro Massacre," carried out by US forces during their ostensible "liberation" of the Philippines from Spanish rule:

A tribe of Moros, dark-skinned savages, had fortified themselves in the bowl of an extinct crater not many miles from Jolo; and as they were hostiles, and bitter against us because we have been trying for eight years to take their liberties away from them, their presence in that position was a menace. Our commander, Gen. Leonard Wood, ordered a reconnaissance. It was found that the Moros numbered six hundred, counting women and children; that their crater bowl was in the summit of a peak or mountain twenty-two hundred feet above sea level, and very difficult of access for Christian troops and artillery.

Then General Wood ordered a surprise, and went along himself to see the order carried out. Our troops climbed the heights by devious and difficult trails, and even took some artillery with them. The kind of artillery is not specified, but in one place it was hoisted up a sharp acclivity by tackle a distance of some three hundred feet. Arrived at the rim of the crater, the battle began. Our soldiers numbered five hundred and forty. They were assisted by auxiliaries consisting of a detachment of native constabulary in our pay—their numbers not given— and by a naval detachment, whose numbers are not stated. But apparently the contending parties were about equal as to number—six hundred men on our side, on the edge of the bowl; six hundred men, women and children in the bottom of the bowl. Depth of the bowl, 50 feet.

Gen. Wood's order was, "Kill or capture the six hundred."

The battle began—it is officially called by that name—our forces firing down into the crater with their artillery and their deadly small arms of precision; the savages furiously returning the fire, probably with brickbats—though this is merely a surmise of mine, as the weapons used by the savages are not nominated in the cablegram. Heretofore the Moros have used knives and clubs mainly; also ineffectual trade-muskets when they had any.

The official report stated that the battle was fought with prodigious energy on both sides during a day and a half, and that it ended with a complete victory for the American arms. The completeness of the victory is established by this fact: that of the six hundred Moros not one was left alive. The brilliancy of the victory is established by this other fact, to wit: that of our six hundred heroes only fifteen lost their lives.

General Wood was present and looking on. His order had been, "Kill or capture those savages." Apparently our little army considered that the "or" left them authorized to kill or capture according to taste, and that their taste had remained what it has been for eight years, in our army out there—the taste of Christian butchers.

The official report quite properly extolled and magnified the "heroism" and "gallantry" of our troops; lamented the loss of the fifteen who perished, and elaborated the wounds of thirty-two of our men who suffered injury, and even minutely and faithfully described the nature of the wounds, in the interest of future historians of the United States. It mentioned that a private had one of his elbows scraped by a missile, and the private's name was mentioned. Another private had the end of his nose scraped by a missile. His name was also mentioned—by cable, at one dollar and fifty cents a word.

What is remarkable about this piece is that it could have been written many years later to talk about US "liberation" interventions in such countries as Korea, Vietnam, and Iraq where the US, with incredibly superior firepower, killed untold numbers of people, mostly civilians, at will and like fish in a barrel, while suffering relatively much fewer casualties. And the reason that the numbers of the victims of US intervention are "untold" is because, as Twain explains, the US only counts, names, and honors its own dead, for they are the only ones worth counting.

Mark Twain had originally supported the Spanish-American War which the US invasion of the Philippines grew out of, believing, as told first by President William McKinley who started the conflict, and then by our revered "rough rider" and president, Teddy Roosevelt, that it was indeed a project to free the peoples of Cuba and the Philippines from Spanish oppression. I also recall learning in high school that this was the goal and indeed the outcome of this glorious war, and that Cuba and the Philippines were in fact democratized by the US intervention.

But the reality, as Twain was honest enough to see and to write about, was quite different.

The fact was that one overlord was replaced by another in this war, and that was the point all along. In the case of Cuba, moreover, the people were well under way to liberating themselves from the Spanish (about two-thirds of the way) when the US intervened to "help" them in 1898, and the US took the opportunity to effectively annex Cuba in the process.[16]

Thus, while initially occupying Cuba from 1898 to 1902, President Roosevelt left Cuba after putting in place the Platt Amendment to Cuba's new constitution. Contrary to the Cuban's desire to have a new Constitution to protect their basic rights and liberties, the Platt Amendment forced upon them gave the US the right "to supervise Cuba's finances and internal development and to intervene militarily to enforce order and stability. . . . The spoils of victory also included a naval base at Guantanamo Bay and the annexation of Puerto Rico."[17]

And so began the US's imperial domination of huge swaths of the world in the name of democracy, freedom, and Jesus.

As for the Philippines, the US treatment of its people—which even included waterboarding, then known as the "water cure"— even shocked and upset some US military commanders.[18] As one commentator recently explained:

> When America defeated Spain in 1898, Filipinos thought three centuries of colonialism were over. They declared the birth of a republic, wrote a constitution, and formed a government under the leadership of Emilio Aguinaldo. But by the terms of the Treaty of Paris, which ended the war, America took possession of the over 7,600 islands that make up the Philippines by paying Spain $20 million for them.
>
> Perhaps unsurprisingly, many Filipinos were outraged. The Philippine-American war that followed from 1899–1902

is considered by many historians to be the first counterinsurgency fought by the US The war featured guerrilla warfare by the Filipinos and, on the American side, "concentration zones," scorched earth tactics, retaliation, and torture. . . .

In the face of all the controversy, the Roosevelt administration declared victory in 1902. 4,200 US soldiers and 20,000 Filipino soldiers were dead. Civilian casualties have been estimated from 250,000–750,000. The White House valorized US troops, but it was the US military's own who begged to differ with the White House. The Commanding General of the US Army's report found that the American use of torture was systemic and the result of a breakdown of moral order.[19]

As for the total number of Filipinos killed, the above-quoted figure is most likely way too small. More credible estimates put the number killed at around three million, or a full one-third of the population, warranting the application of the term "genocide" to the American slaughter.[20] In any case, what is clear is that the only "liberating" that US forces carried out in the Philippines was freeing many poor souls from their mortal coil.

In short order, the US would invade other countries, particularly in the Caribbean. For example, in 1915, the great promoter of democracy and international law, President Woodrow Wilson—after whom Princeton's world-renowned international diplomacy school is still named—ordered the invasion of Haiti. Even before this invasion, the US had been intervening in Haiti. Most notably, "when the slaves in the country fought for independence in the late eighteenth century, the US provided aid to the French colonists in an effort to stop the rebellion, fearful that the revolt would spread to the US."[21] And, when the independence movement in Haiti finally succeeded, in spite of the US's best efforts, the US withheld recognition of the new Haitian government for sixty years in retaliation for its premature outlawing of slavery.[22]

Through the 1915 invasion, the US brought liberty to the people of Haiti by reestablishing forced labor, putting them on chain gangs to build roads and infrastructure to support US business concerns; looting the Haitian bank of all its cash and gold reserves and dissolving its democratically elected legislature for refusing to adopt a constitution allowing for foreign land ownership.[23] The US would not withdraw its troops until 1934. All told, about fifteen thousand Haitians were killed in the three first years of the resistance to the invasion in which, according to one of the leaders of the US campaign, General Smedley Butler, the rebels were "'hunted down . . . like pigs.'"[24]

These brutal international forays were justified back then by the Monroe Doctrine, a seemingly benign policy of opposing European colonization over our southern neighbors residing in "our backyard," and the less discussed Roosevelt corollary thereto pursuant to which Teddy Roosevelt declared the right to exercise "international police power" in the Western Hemisphere and beyond.[25] The US relied upon these doctrines to justify thirty interventions in the Caribbean in the first three decades of the twentieth century.[26]

Today, we hardly hear the term Monroe Doctrine, and even less so the Roosevelt corollary, as they are seen as largely outdated, and many of the quite brutal actions carried out pursuant to them best forgotten. Most honest people today, if they knew about or gave much thought to this history, would recognize that this epoch in US foreign policy was nothing other than naked colonialism.

Even General Smedley Butler himself, who hunted Haitians and many others down "like pigs," was honest enough to admit this later, famously explaining:

> I spent 33 years and four months in active military service and during that period I spent most of my time as a high class muscle man for Big Business, for Wall Street and the bankers.

In short, I was a racketeer, a gangster for capitalism. I helped make Mexico and especially Tampico safe for American oil interests in 1914. I helped make Haiti and Cuba a decent place for the National City Bank boys to collect revenues in. I helped in the raping of half a dozen Central American republics for the benefit of Wall Street. I helped purify Nicaragua for the International Banking House of Brown Brothers in 1902–1912. I brought light to the Dominican Republic for the American sugar interests in 1916. I helped make Honduras right for the American fruit companies in 1903. In China in 1927 I helped see to it that Standard Oil went on its way unmolested. Looking back on it, I might have given Al Capone a few hints. The best he could do was to operate his racket in three districts. I operated on three continents.[27]

The brilliant trick US leaders have always managed to pull off has been to convince the public that we would never engage in such brazen acts of aggression; that to the extent we have, it has been aberrational, inadvertent, and certainly unintentional; and that now, from here on out, we will really live up to our true mandate of spreading democracy and freedom everywhere. Then, when everyone is well-convinced of this laudable intention and lulled into sleepy complacency, the same leaders immediately come up with another convincing justification, draped up in lofty goals and rhetoric, to continue the very same policies of imperialist intervention as before.

And so, after WWII, President Harry S. Truman came up with his famous Truman Doctrine which would be in effect until at least 1989 and the end of the Cold War. Pursuant to this Doctrine, the US claimed the right to intervene economically, politically, and militarily around the world to halt the spread of Communism.[28] With this announcement, the beginning of the Cold War officially began.

As the noted historian Odd Arne Westad correctly pointed out, however, "the Cold War was a continuation of colonialism through slightly different means."[29] And indeed, the "Kennan Corollary" to the Truman Doctrine was quite upfront about this. Thus, George F. Kennan, one of the chief architects of the Cold War doctrine which would be in effect for nearly fifty years, announced that the US must continue its dominion, particularly over Latin America, with the goal of protecting "access to 'our' raw materials" and ensuring the respect for the US's special role in the world.[30]

Kennan, who toured Latin America and felt utter contempt for the people, religion, and culture he encountered there, concluded that "'harsh governmental measures of repression may be the only answer; that these measures may have to proceed from regimes whose origins and methods would not stand the test of American concerns of democratic procedures; and that such regimes and such methods may be preferable alternatives, to further communist successes.'"[31] Jeane Kirkpatrick, in her famous 1979 *Commentary* piece, articulated the very same ideas, stating that the US should unapologetically support right-wing dictatorships in the Third World, such as those of the Shah of Iran and Somoza of Nicaragua, in order to protect our interests. This would become known as the Kirkpatrick Doctrine, and Reagan would follow it with great élan.

Meanwhile, this new form of colonialism would often be carried out through the CIA in more covert and subtle ways than before, but with equally devastating consequences. As suggested by Kennan and later Kirkpatrick, this many times meant partnering with extreme right-wing, fascist, and even Nazi forces to get the job done. And of course, this made perfect sense for President Harry Truman who himself had famously proclaimed his indifference during WWII as to whether the Nazis or the Soviets won the war; either way, the goal was to make sure that the US came out on top of everyone.

And, Truman would get down to business right away. Quite befittingly, he would begin his project of intervention in the cradle of democracy and Western civilization itself—Greece. In 1947, Greece was being ruled by a fascist/monarchist government which was reinstalled by Great Britain after being toppled by a popular struggle during WWII.[32] Great Britain, feeling exhausted by WWII, now called upon the US to help militarily prop up the retrograde government against a left-wing guerilla movement which, all agree now, was indigenous, and not being supported by the Soviet Union.

As the US State Department Office of the Historian explains, "[i]n fact, Soviet leader Joseph Stalin had deliberately refrained from providing any support to the Greek Communists and had forced Yugoslav Prime Minister Josip Tito to follow suit, much to the detriment of Soviet-Yugoslav relations."[33] But again, what the people of Greece wanted themselves was completely irrelevant, despite a new UN Charter which enshrined the right of nations to choose their own political and economic systems.

Answering the call, Truman came to the rescue, requesting $400 million from Congress to help in the struggle to keep the fascists in control in Greece. As Howard Zinn explains:

> The United States moved into the Greek civil war, not with soldiers, but with weapons and military advisers. In the last five months of 1947, 74,000 tons of military equipment were sent by the United States to the right-wing government in Athens, including artillery, dive bombers, and stocks of napalm. Two hundred and fifty army officers, headed by General James Van Fleet, advised the Greek army in the field. Van Fleet started a policy—standard in dealing with popular insurrections of forcibly removing thousands of Greeks from their homes in the countryside, to try to isolate the guerrillas, to remove the source of their support.[34]

As Zinn also explained, the control of regional oil sources was also behind this military intervention, but that was never a point Truman mentioned. In the end, the US helped make Greek safe for fascism once again. And, the regime reinstalled in Greece "instituted a highly brutal regime, for which the CIA created a suitably repressive internal security agency (KYP in Greek)."[35] The fascist government erected a statue of Harry S. Truman in Athens as thanks for the US's role in the coup under his leadership. This statue has been blown up, rebuilt, and blown up again several times.

However, all good things must come to an end. And so, much to the chagrin of both Britain and the US, democracy broke out again when liberal George Papandreou was elected in 1964. Just before the 1967 elections which Papandreou was sure to win again, a joint effort of Britain, the CIA, Greek Military, KYP, and US military stationed in Greece brought about a military coup which brought the fascists back to power. And, the new rightist government immediately instituted "martial law, censorship, arrests, beatings, and killing, the victims totaling eight thousand in the first month. . . . Torture, inflicted in the most gruesome ways, often with equipment supplied by the United States, became routine."[36] All was right with the world once more.

Meanwhile, Truman and his successors made sure that rightists and fascists regained power elsewhere in the world. And so, for example, after using nuclear weapons to end the war against imperial Japan in WWII (or quite possibly to begin the new war against the USSR), the US moved quickly to reinstate the very people we had defeated. As the *New York Times* explained years later:

> In a major covert operation of the cold war, the Central Intelligence Agency spent millions of dollars to support the conservative party that dominated Japan's politics for a generation.

The C.I.A. gave money to the Liberal Democratic Party and its members in the 1950's and the 1960's, to gather intelligence on Japan, make the country a bulwark against Communism in Asia and undermine the Japanese left, said retired intelligence officials and former diplomats.[37]

As the *NYT* explains, "the payments to the party and its politicians were 'so established and so routine' that they were a fundamental, if highly secret, part of American foreign policy toward Japan . . . ." The result of this interference was, as all admit today, the creation of a corrupt, "one-party conservative" state. The *NYT* refers to this as a "one-party, conservative democracy," but that, of course, is a contradiction in terms.

And, what the *NYT* does not mention is that the leader the US initially selected to secure its interests in Japan and the Pacific was Nobusuke Kishi, also known as the "Shōwa (Emperor) era monster/devil"—the war criminal, famous for his brutality, who oversaw the use of coerced Korean and Chinese labor in Japan's Manchurian munitions factories.[38] The US exonerated Kishi for his WWII-era war crimes, and, with the critical assistance of the CIA, he went on to serve two terms as Japan's prime minister in the 1950s, becoming widely known as "America's favorite war criminal."[39]

The US, again through the CIA, did the very same in Italy, successfully influencing the outcome of elections there for nearly a quarter of a century. Again, the *New York Times*, citing former CIA officer, F. Mark Wyatt, explains:

Mr. Wyatt joined the C.I.A.'s clandestine service in 1948, months after the agency's birth, and plunged into its first successful covert effort. The mission was to ensure the electoral victory of Italy's Christian Democrats over the Communist Party.

Mr. Wyatt helped deliver millions of dollars to the eventual victors; the precise cost of the covert campaign has never been declassified, though the details of the operation were.

"We had bags of money that we delivered to selected politicians, to defray their political expenses, their campaign expenses, for posters, for pamphlets," Mr. Wyatt said in a 1995 interview recorded for "Cold War," a 1998 documentary shown on CNN. Suitcases filled with cash had changed hands in the four-star Hotel Hassler in Rome, he said. The Christian Democrats won the elections by a comfortable margin and formed a government that excluded the Communists.

The C.I.A.'s practice of buying political clout was repeated in every Italian election for the next 24 years, and the agency's political influence in Rome lasted a generation, declassified records show.[40]

Moreover, in addition to propping up the Christian Democratic Party with millions of dollars in cash, "CIA operatives . . . helped orchestrate what was then an unprecedented, clandestine propaganda campaign: This included forging documents to besmirch communist leaders via fabricated sex scandals, starting a mass letter-writing campaign from Italian Americans to their compatriots, and spreading hysteria about a Russian takeover and the undermining of the Catholic Church."[41]

Meanwhile, the US would seamlessly continue to intervene and subvert democracy in such countries as Cuba, the Philippines, and Haiti.

In terms of Cuba, the US, in the interest of keeping the island safe from Communism and safe for US businesses (including the lucrative gambling industry) would provide unconditional "political, moral, economic, and military support" to the "corrupt, repressive" dictator Fulgencio Batista from 1952 until 1959 when he was finally overthrown by guerilla forces led by Fidel

Castro.[42] And, the US has never stopped intervening since, even decades after the end of the Cold War and the collapse of the Soviet Union, engaging in an endless series of "terrorist attacks, bombings, full-scale military invasion, sanctions, embargoes, isolation, assassinations,"[43] and hundreds of assassination attempts against Fidel Castro himself. Moreover, contrary to the overwhelming desire of the Cuban people, the US continues to control the Naval Base at Guantanamo Bay which, of course, it also uses as a detention center and torture chamber.

In the Philippines, the US, after abandoning the islands to the fate of the brutal Japanese invasion for most of WWII, supported the repressive and corrupt dictatorship of Ferdinand Marcos from 1965 to 1983.[44] The US viewed Marcos as an important bulwark against the spread of Communism (in reality decolonization) in South East Asia, especially given that he was one of the few regional leaders willing to support the US war effort in Vietnam.

The US supported him through his most repressive years in the 1970s when he declared Martial Rule. As *Agence France-Presse* explains:

> By doing so he could stay in power longer than the constitutionally mandated limit of eight years.
>
> With the continued backing of the United States, the Philippines' former colonial ruler, Marcos ruthlessly moved to stamp out dissent.
>
> Television, radio stations and newspapers were only allowed to promote his "New Society," so the public was fed a constant stream of praise for Marcos and his jet-setting wife, whose extravagance was a sharp contrast to the poverty of most Filipinos.
>
> Opposition politicians, including Marcos arch-critic Senator Benigno Aquino, as well as student leaders and

other dissidents, were thrown behind bars, as the Philippines descended into a climate of fear.

"The Marcos government appears, by any standard, exceptional for both the quantity and quality of its violence," wrote American academic Alfred McCoy, one of the pre-eminent historians on the Philippines.

McCoy said the regime's security forces killed 3,257 people—many of the victims first abducted, then abused and finally murdered and dumped on a roadside in a warning to others.

An additional 35,000 were tortured and 70,000 were unfairly imprisoned under Marcos, according to McCoy.[45]

As far as the US was concerned, however, all was fair in love and war on Communism, or at least perceived Communism, and democracy in the Philippines could always wait for another day.

But it is Haiti which the US has treated with particular cruelty. The US has never in reality allowed Haiti to govern itself. Thus, the US did not withdraw the Marines from Haiti before creating and arming "'a modern army, one that would continue the US occupation long after US troops were gone', functioning on behalf of the Haitian elite and their American counterparts. . . . 'The US occupation wedded the country's future to North American business interests.'"[46]

Then, from 1957 to 1986, the US would economically and militarily support the brutal dictatorships of Francois "Papa Doc" Duvalier and his son Jean-Claude "Baby Doc" Duvalier. To help "Papa Doc" stay in power, "US Marines trained the dictator's Tonton Macoutes paramilitary force, known for 'leaving bodies of their victims hanging in public, a clear warning to anyone stepping out of line, most especially leftists, socialists and pro-democracy activists.'"[47] US Marine instructors, "who were working through a company . . . under contract with the CIA and

signed off by the US State Department,'" then trained the paramilitary group known as the Leopards for "Baby Doc" Duvalier.[48]

Just after the fall of the "Baby" Doc dictatorship, the CIA
helped to create the appropriately named S.I.N., short for the
National Intelligence Service of Haiti. As the *New York Times*,
referring to the S.I.N., would later explain, "[t]he Central
Intelligence Agency created an intelligence service in Haiti in the
mid-1980's to fight the cocaine trade, but the unit evolved into
an instrument of political terror whose officers at times engaged
in drug trafficking . . . ."[49] The depths of S.I.N.'s corruption was
staggering. As the *Times* wrote:

> The Haitian intelligence service provided little information on
> drug trafficking and some of its members themselves became
> enmeshed in the drug trade, American officials said. A United
> States official who worked at the American Embassy in Haiti in
> 1991 and 1992 said he took a dim view of S.I.N.
>
> "It was a military organization that distributed drugs in
> Haiti," said the official, who spoke on condition of anonymity.
> "It never produced drug intelligence. The agency gave them
> money under counternarcotics and they used their training to
> do other things in the political arena."

Still, the CIA support kept coming. Thus, the "S.I.N. received
$500,000 to $1 million a year in equipment, training and financial support from the C.I.A," and it received this assistance to
and through the time the S.I.N. engaged in its most notorious
act "in the political arena"—the successful overthrew of the democratically elected president, Father Jean-Bertrand Aristide, on
September 30, 1991. Moreover, the US Drug Enforcement Agency
said of the S.I.A. as late as 1992 that it "'works in unison with the
C.I.A. at post.'"

That Father Aristide was overthrown by CIA-backed forces

came as little surprise to most observers. Aristide has always been seen as a problem for the US in the region given his advocacy of Liberation Theology whose main tenet is "the preferential treatment for the poor." Even worse, Aristide tried hard to put this philosophy into practice as president. As one commentator wrote:

> Aristide's coup-inducing crimes included inviting street children and homeless persons to breakfast at the National Palace and endeavouring to raise the daily minimum wage from $1.76 to $2.94. As Joanne Landy wrote in the *New York Times* in 1994, the latter effort was "vigorously opposed by the US Agency for International Development because of the threat such an increase would pose to the 'business climate', particularly to American companies paying rock-bottom wages to workers in Haiti".[50]

Even after the coup against Aristide, the CIA, along with the US Defense Intelligence Agency (DIA), continued to organize and work with repressive forces to ensure that Haiti would be a safe haven for sweatshops. One such force was the euphemistically named Front for the Advancement and Progress of Haiti (FRAPH), a paramilitary organization intimately linked to the Haitian military that assumed the task of terrorizing the non-elite masses under the military junta which ruled after the coup.[51]

Again, the *New York Times*, invariably writing well after the fact, explained that Emmanuel Constant, "[t]he leader of one of Haiti's most infamous paramilitary groups [FRAPH] was a paid informer of the Central Intelligence Agency for two years and was receiving money from the United States while his associates committed political murders and other acts of repression . . . ."[52] The FRAPH chief was even on the CIA payroll, the *Times* explains, at the time the FRAPH was organizing violent protests to try to prevent the return to office of Father Aristide in 1994.

President Bill Clinton actually assisted Aristide in returning to office in 1994, even as his own CIA was working against these plans. However, Clinton's intervention in this regard was not altruistic—far from it. Rather, Clinton paved the way for Aristide's return on the express condition that Aristide make drastic changes to Haiti's agricultural system in order to benefit US, and in particular, Arkansas farmers. These changes, which required Haiti to import thousands of tons of rice, would be ruinous to the country, undercutting Haiti's ability to feed itself and resulting in millions of Haitians starving.[53] Clinton himself would later admit to this. As *Foreign Policy* explained:

> In the wake of Haiti's devastating 7.0-magnitude earthquake exactly three years ago, former US President Bill Clinton issued an unusual and now infamous apology. Calling his subsidies to American rice farmers in the 1990s a mistake because it undercut rice production in Haiti, Clinton said he had struck a "devil's bargain" that ultimately resulted in greater poverty and food insecurity in Haiti.
>
> "It may have been good for some of my farmers in Arkansas, but it has not worked," he said. "I have to live every day with the consequences of the lost capacity to produce a rice crop in Haiti to feed those people, because of what I did."[54]

However, the US continued to be worried about Aristide who disbanded the Haitian military—a military which had protected US interests for so long. Therefore, shortly after Aristide was elected as president for a third time in 2001, the US began to destabilize Haiti.

First, "[i]n 2002, the US stopped hundreds of millions of dollars in loans to Haiti which were to be used for, among other public projects like education, roads."[55] And then, in early 2003, the US encouraged paramilitary incursions into Haiti from the neighboring Dominican Republic which ultimately led to the toppling of Aristide again. These paramilitaries were led by Andre Apaid, who "was in touch with US Secretary of State Colin Powell in the weeks leading up to Aristide's overthrow," and by Guy Philippe and former FRAPH leader Emmanuel Constant, both who "had ties to the CIA, and were in touch with US officials" during this time.[56]

In 2004, the US then moved in, along with France and Canada, to remove Aristide in the name of restoring peace and order to Haiti—the peace and order which the US had helped to destroy in the first place. As one commentator put it succinctly, Aristide's "inability to maintain order in an atmosphere of US-backed destabilization had provided an excellent pretext for another exercise in 'regime change.'" Aristide was "kidnapped at gunpoint" by the joint US, France, and Canadian forces, and "flown without his knowledge to the Central African Republic" on a US military aircraft.[57]

As the *Huffington Post* explained in a postmortem of the coup, "[i]n 2004, the US again destroyed democracy in Haiti . . . ."[58] Between 2004 and 2006, Haiti was ruled by Gerard Latortue. And during these two years, with Aristide gone, and peace and order restored, "Haiti experienced some 4,000 political murders, according to The Lancet - while hundreds of Fanmi Lavalas members, Aristide supporters, and social movement leaders were locked up - usually on bogus charges. Latortue's friends in Washington looked the other way."[59] Haiti's democracy has not recovered. Indeed, "Haiti has remained rocked by political turmoil in the years since . . . ."[60]

Haiti represents an emblematic case of US intervention over a large expanse of time. While the specific, claimed justifications for intervention changed over time—e.g., opposing the end of slavery, enforcing the Monroe Doctrine, fighting Communism, fighting drugs, restoring law and order—the fact is that the

interventions never stopped and the results for the Haitian people have been invariably disastrous. In the end, the true goal of
all of these interventions was, and shall always be, the protection
of US economic interests.

But they will always be dressed up in the packaging of loft-
ier aspirations, making the interventions more palatable to the
American people who have never given up on the idea that God
has ordained us to rule the world, and that such rule is, by its
nature, good and right. The following descriptions of other
emblematic interventions, though hardly exhaustive, demonstrate this same pattern of the exercise so many believe to be our
Manifest Destiny.

2

RUSSIA 1996:
MAKING THE COUNTRY SAFE
FOR PLUNDER

IT IS NOW GENERALLY ACCEPTED THAT the US, under President
Bill Clinton, heavily interfered in the pivotal 1996 election in
Russia on behalf of the terribly unpopular Boris Yeltsin who was
seeking a second term as president. Indeed, the foregoing *NYT*
article on US election meddling explains, "American fears that
Boris Yeltsin would be defeated for reelection as president in 1996
by an old-fashioned Communist led to an overt and covert effort
to help him, urged on by President Bill Clinton. It included an
American push for a $10 billion International Monetary Fund
loan to Russia four months before the voting and a team of
American political consultants . . . ."

The study in Oxford University's *International Studies
Quarterly* also lists the 1996 Russian election as one in which the
US engaged in "overt" election interference.

However, before we get to 1996, it may be worth looking at
events in the more distant path. As we continue to receive our
daily dose of Russia bashing by much of the US press, it is worth
remembering that while Russia has never invaded the United
States, the US did in fact invade Russia without provocation
shortly after its 1917 Revolution. President Wilson, wanting to
make the world safe for capitalism, attempted to strangle this

socialist revolution in its crib by coming to the aid of quite ruth-less counterrevolutionary forces in that country.

As recounted by Jeremy Kuzamarov and John Marciano in their recent book, *The Russians are Coming, Again*:

> President Wilson deployed over ten thousand American troops to the European theater of the First World War, alongside British, French, Canadian, and Japanese troops, in support of the White Army counter-revolutionary generals implicated in wide-scale atrocities, including pogroms against Jews. . . .
>
> The atrocities associated with this war and the trampling on Soviet Russia's sovereignty would remain seared in its peo-ple's memory, shaping a deep sense of mistrust that carries into the present day. . . .

Kuzamarov and Marciano then quote historian D.F. Fleming, who Harold Pinter seemed to echo in his Nobel Prize speech: "'For the American people, the cosmic tragedy of the intervention in Russia does not exist, or it was an unimportant incident, long forgotten. But for the Soviet people and their leaders the period was a time of endless killing, of looting and raping, of plague and famine, of measureless suffering for scores of millions—an experience burned into the very soul of the nation, not to be for-gotten for many generations, if ever. Also, for many years, the harsh Soviet regimentation could all be justified by fear that the Capitalist power would be back to finish the job.'" And in fact, that power would be back to finish the job as soon as it saw its opportunity.

That moment came after the collapse of the USSR in 1991, and the ascendancy of Boris Yeltsin to the presidency. The US was able to prevail upon Yeltsin to impose the harshest of eco-nomic policies upon the Russian people—policies which would immiserate the Russian population, but which would at the same time prevent any restoration of socialism and which would allow for the maximum plunder of the economy built up under the USSR.

As Russian Scholar Stephen F. Cohen explains in his important work, *Soviet Fates And Lost Alternatives*,[61] post-Soviet Russia under the stewardship of Yeltsin suffered a major economic collapse, with investment in the economy falling by 80 percent, and 75 percent of the population falling into poverty. As Cohen explains, Russia became "the first nation to ever undergo actual de-modernization in peacetime." Cohen relates that this led one Moscow philosopher to state, in regard to those who long wanted to destroy the Soviet Union, "They were aiming at Communism but hitting Russia."

As explained in a study conducted by the National Center for Biotechnology Information (NCBI), "[t]he changes in Russian mortality in the 1990s are unprecedented in a modern industrialized country in peacetime." In this study, the NCBI estimated that, between 1992–2001, there were approximately 2.5 to 3 million premature Russian deaths as a result of the combination of the economic and social dislocation caused by the collapse of the USSR and the 1998 economic crisis which followed.[62] Other Western demographers have put the total excess deaths at between five and six million, while Professor of Sociology James Petras puts the figure at fifteen million.[63]

This devastating collapse in post-Soviet Russia was overseen and managed, or mismanaged to be more precise, by Yeltsin who, in turn, took his cues from President Bill Clinton.

In a Congressional Research Service (CRS) Report, entitled, "Russian Political Turmoil,"[64] Russia's economic crisis of the 1992 to 1998 period "can be traced . . . ultimately to [Boris] Yeltsin . . . under whose stewardship the GDP has contracted by 50%, accompanied by economic distress worse than the Great Depression of the 1930s in the United States for most of the Russian population."

And, as the CRS Report continues, even when Yeltsin's administration "assembled a western-oriented economic team and pursued economic policies supported by the Clinton Administration,
the G-7, and the IMF . . . economic conditions and the government's and Yeltsin's approval ratings continued to deteriorate."

The Report goes on to admit that "[s]ome critics of US policy
toward Russia charge that it is too closely linked to Yeltsin and is
seen by ordinary Russians as endorsing Yeltsin and the unpopular economic policies that they blame for leading the country to
ruin." On the other hand, the Report states, "[d]efenders of US
policy reply that Yeltsin has steered Russia on an essentially correct, *though painful*, course." (emphasis added). In other words,
regardless which side one was on in this debate, there was no
questioning the fact that the course supported by the US was
"painful" for the Russian people. But, the argument went, the
Russian people's pain was potentially our gain, given that "[a]
weak and unstable Russia may be less likely to pose an aggressive
military threat . . . ."

The man to continue Russia's pain and unraveling was Boris
Yeltsin. And the Clinton White House would make sure that he
would win a second term in office despite the Russian people's
quite predictable distain for his policies.

As a July 15, 1996, *Time* magazine article entitled, "Rescuing
Boris," detailed,[65] this meant sending in a team of US political
consultants who were paid $250,000 plus expenses to secretly
manage and redirect Yeltsin's failing 1996 presidential campaign.
This team included Dick Morris, Bill Clinton's chief campaign
adviser, and Richard Dresner, who had helped with Bill Clinton's
electoral victories for Arkansas Governor.

In addition, as Dick Morris would later explain, President
Bill Clinton himself acted as key adviser to Yeltsin. As Morris
recently explained, "We, Clinton and I, would go through it and
Bill would pick up the hotline and talk to Yeltsin and tell him

what commercials to run, where to campaign, what positions to take. He basically became Yeltsin's political consultant."

The help given by the Clinton White House, including its ensuring the $10 billion "emergency infusion" of IMF monies to Russia shortly before the election[66]—$1 billion of which was directly earmarked for Yeltsin's reelection campaign[67]—was absolutely critical. As *Time* magazine explained, Yeltsin was deeply unpopular with the Russian people given "his brutal misadventure in Chechnya; his increasing authoritarianism; and his economic reform program, which has brought about corruption and widespread suffering." Indeed, Yeltsin, had a 6 percent approval rating at the time the American consultants intervened.[68]

Ultimately, however, Boris was rescued by the Clinton White House. In return, it should be noted, Clinton was able to get something in return for one of his old Arkansas buddies and major campaign donors, Tyson Chicken, prevailing upon Yeltsin to exempt Tyson from 20 percent tariffs which otherwise would have been imposed on its chicken imports.[69]

The *Time* magazine article concluded in a triumphant tone, explaining that, with Yeltsin's ultimate nail-biter of a win, "Democracy triumphed—and along with it came the tools of modern campaigns, including the trickery and slickery Americans know so well."

Examples of the American "trickery and slickery" which Yeltsin used to win reelection were "extensive 'black operations,' including disrupting opposition rallies and press conferences, spreading disinformation among Yeltsin supporters, and denying media access to the opposition."[70] The dirty tricks also included such tactics as announcing false dates for opposition rallies and press conferences, disseminating alarming campaign materials that they deceitfully attributed to the [opposition] Zyuganov campaign, and cancelling hotel reservations for Zyuganov and his volunteers.[71]

Finally, widespread bribery, voter fraud, intimidation, and ballot stuffing assured Yeltsin's ultimate victory in the presidential vote which had to go to a runoff election because it was so close—that is, if Yeltsin really won at all. Thus, then-President Dimitri Medvedev told attendees at a closed-door meeting in 2012 that "Russia's first President did not actually win re-election in 1996 for a second term. The second presidential vote in Russia's history, in other words, was rigged."[72]

Meanwhile, buried in the *Time* magazine article was a reference to "the Duma catastrophe," which the article also cited as an event that made Yeltsin's reelection bid so difficult. It is worth revisiting what this "catastrophe" was as it illustrates what kind of "democrat" Yeltsin really was, and reveals just as much about the US which continues to hold Yelstin up as a pillar of democracy.

In short, "the Duma catastrophe" began with a political stand-off between the Duma—the Russian legislature, and at the time the most powerful branch of Russian government—and Boris Yeltsin. The Duma, which still had a large contingent of Communists who were resistant to the market changes which were, by all accounts, wreaking havoc in Russia, was refusing to approve Yeltsin's pick for prime minister, Yegor Gaidar. As one publication explains, "Gaidar, who was the architect of the economic shock therapy and Yeltsin, who backed the plan, were vastly unpopular among the Russian public at the time, which encouraged the decision of the Duma leaders to act against the executive branch."[73]

In other words, the legislators were being asked by their constituents to resist an unpopular president, just as the Democrats are now being urged to resist Trump.

In response, Yeltsin tried to dissolve the Duma, but the Duma declared this action to be unconstitutional. They then proceeded to remove Yeltsin from office and to install the vice president in his stead. Yeltsin responded by shutting off electricity and water to the

White House, which then housed the Duma. And, when a number of Duma lawmakers still refused to leave and supporters showed up to the White House to protest Yeltsin's actions, Yeltsin did what any good, democratic leader would do: he shelled the Russian White House, killing anywhere between two hundred and two thousand people.[74] A new Constitution was then adopted which gave more power to the Executive Branch. In the end, these "events that took place on October 1993 secured the domination of the executive branch over the legislative and judicial branches, effectively prohibiting the country from being a parliamentary republic."[75]

As I remember quite vividly from that time, the actions of Yeltsin in bombing his own legislative building and assuming greater power was applauded by both Washington and the US media as a triumph for Russian democracy. In this event—reminiscent of the "Tiananmen Square massacre" in China just four years before in which three hundred to three thousand people were killed[76]—the West was rooting for the tanks.

As Stephen F. Cohen explains, the Russian people, not surprisingly, characterized the deeply flawed reign of Yeltsin as "shit-ocracy," and they naturally welcomed a change in the person of Vladimir Putin who was, and is viewed, as being able to bring back order, stability, and national pride to Russia.[77]

David Satter, writing for the *Wall Street Journal*, explained it succinctly: "Yeltsin . . . and the small group of economists who advised him, decided that the most urgent priority for Russia was putting property immediately into private hands, even if those hands were criminal. In this, they were fully supported by the US. The result was that the path was laid for the pillaging of the country and the rise in Russia" of Putin.

Meanwhile, it is worth remembering, as US officials and media fret about Vladimir Putin's conduct in the former Soviet Republic of Ukraine, that the Clinton administration also showed no tangible concern for Yeltsin's prosecution of the first

of a brutal war in the Chechen War Republic. As Helsinki Watch
(now Human Rights Watch) reported at the time:

> Russian forces prosecuted a brutal war in the breakaway repub-
> lic of Chechnya with total disregard for humanitarian law,
> causing thousands of needless civilian casualties. . . .
>
> Russian President Boris Yeltsin ordered 40,000 troops to
> Chechnya on December 11, 1994, to stop that republic's bid for
> independence. A December 17, 1994, government statement
> promised that "force [in Chechnya] will be employed with due
> consideration of the principle of humanity." But within one
> week Russian forces began bombing Grozny, Chechnya's capi-
> tal, in a campaign unparalleled in the area since World War II
> for its scope and destructiveness, followed by months of indis-
> criminate and targeted fire against civilians. Russian Human
> Rights Commissioner Sergei Kovalyev, who remained in
> Grozny through much of the bombing, bore personal witness
> to the destruction of homes, hospitals, schools, orphanages and
> other civilian structures. Indiscriminate bombing and shelling
> killed civilians and destroyed civilian property not only in
> Grozny but also in other regions in Chechnya, especially in the
> southern mountain areas.[78]

Helsinki Watch complained that "[t]he Clinton administration responded sluggishly to the slaughter in Chechnya and
failed to link Russian conduct with important concessions, such
as the May summit with President Yeltsin or support for IMF
loans."[79] To the contrary, as noted above, Clinton prevailed upon
the IMF to give a massive infusion of money to Russia in the
year this Helsinki Watch report was written in order to guarantee
Boris Yeltsin's reelection.

In the end, there was nothing very democratic about the
Yeltsin regime, and the US, beyond some lip service, did nothing

to coax Yeltsin into being democratic. Indeed, given that the communists in the mid-1990s had much popular support, real democracy in Russia was anathema to the US goal of making sure that Russia was subject to the cruelties of unfettered capitalism.

This is why the Clinton administration even stood by as Yeltsin oversaw passage of "the Law on the Federal Security Service (or FSB, formerly the KGB), which permits the FSB to conduct searches without warrants, conduct their own investigations, arrest suspects, and run their own prisons, suspended fundamental civil rights and restored powers that were among the hallmarks of the Soviet era."[80] Helsinki Watch noted that "[t]his legislative carte blanche is especially alarming since the FSB increasingly has been involved in human rights violations."

The US's indifference to such measures proved once again that it is not repression *per se* which is a problem—not even Soviet-style repression—as long as the West's free market goals are advanced by the repression. And advanced they were. Indeed, as Paul Craig Roberts, former assistant secretary of the Treasury under President Ronald Reagan, explains:

> Remember, the initial collapse of the USSR worked very much to the West's advantage. They could easily manipulate [Boris] Yeltsin, and various oligarchs were able to seize and plunder the resources of the country. Much Israeli and American money was part of that.[81]

Yeltsin has indeed been compared to another favorite of the U.S., Augusto Pinochet, the fascist leader the US installed in Chile in 1973 in order to make sure that social justice would not break out in that country.[82]

3

IRAN

THE CIA'S FIRST FORAY INTO FULL-BLOWN regime change was in Iran in 1953. The target of the CIA's operations was Prime Minister Mohammad who had committed the grave sin of nationalizing its own oil fields which, since 1919, had been controlled by Great Britain for the latter's own benefit and profit.

While Great Britain had profited greatly from Iran's oil, the people of Iran were kept "in a state of squalor unequaled in the world." According to historian D.F. Fleming, in his lost classic *The Origins of the Cold War*, "[i]n some villages 90 percent of the people had malaria, and infant mortality exceeded 50 percent." Iran, according to Fleming, was truly "'a nation in rags.' Abject misery was graven on most faces. Even in Teheran anyone standing on the street would be approached by a beggar every five minutes."

It was against this backdrop that, in the early 1950s, the people of Iran united around a talented, nationalist politician to try to gain true independence—independence which necessarily included more Iranian control over its precious oil resources. The politician's name was Mohammed Mossadegh.

Mossadegh, upon being elected to the Majlis' oil committee, and suspecting that the British were short-changing the Iranians on the oil royalties owed them, initially made the quite reasonable request for the British to open Anglo-Persian's financial books. The British refused this request as well as Mossadegh's request to train Iranians in technical jobs of the oil industry. When Mossadegh was elected head of the Majlis' oil committee, he then demanded that Iran receive half the profits of the Anglo-Persian Oil Company. Again, Britain refused.

It was only after the British refusals of these reasonable requests that the Majlis, under the leadership of Mossadegh who was elected prime minister by overwhelming vote of the Majilis on April 28, 1951, finally decided to nationalize Iran's oil industry on May 1, 1951.

In retaliation, the British stopped exporting refined oil from the Abbadan refinery, and Iran, without tankers or oil technicians of its own, could neither run the refinery nor export any oil. And once Winston Churchill returned as UK prime minister in October of 1951, Britain took even more aggressive action against Mossadegh, buying off Iranian media and undermining the country's economy.[83]

PM Churchill, with the help of CIA chief Allen Dulles, came up with a tried-and-true pitch for getting rid of Mossadegh—claiming an urgent need to rescue Iran and the Middle East from the specter of Communism.[84] This sales point worked like a charm on President Eisenhower who readily green-lighted a US-instigated coup against Mossadegh. The coup plot was dubbed "Operation Ajax."

The coup plot was carried out by the CIA, headed by Allen Dulles, in close coordination with the US State Department, then headed by Allen's brother John, and the White House. It was collectively decided by these groups that they would reinstall the Shah, who Mossadegh had sidelined in the interest of trying to democratize Iran, and replace Mossadegh with General Fazlollah Zahedi in the prime minister position.

General Zahedi was known as a strongman, having been dismissed by Mossadegh from his position as minister of the Interior after he "ordered the massacre" of protestors.[85] Zahedi also had a dark past, having been exiled by the British during WWII as a war profiteer and as a close friend of Nazi agents.

As evidenced in a CIA memo contained in the 2017 released documents, Zahedi's having been a Nazi collaborator was seen as an asset to the Americans. As the memo, detailing US assets in Iran, explains, "[a]ssociated with the Nazi efforts in Iran during World War II, he has long been firmly anti-Soviet. A pro-Western orientation is reflected in the education of his son in the US and the activity of his son in the Point IV [Truman's Cold War technical assistance plan to developing countries] in Iran. . . ." The memo goes on to say that the CIA's assets in Iran believed Zahedi "to be the only military man on the scene who would stage a coup and follow it through with forcefulness."[86]

The game plan the US ran in Iran in 1953 was the standard one it ran during the Cold War—that is, target a nationalist government for overthrow in the interest of preserving US economic domination, and justify such an overthrow by manufacturing a Communist threat. Such a threat is manufactured, as in the case of Iran, by isolating the targeted country economically and politically, starving its economy (or, making "the economy scream" as President Nixon put it in reference to the US's policy toward Chile's Allende government) and thereby pushing that country into the arms of the Soviets. Then, the US could claim that it must overthrow that country's government because of its ties to the Soviets—ties that the US forced upon them.

As for the part of the plan to starve the targeted country's economy, that plan was aggressively followed by the US and Britain in their goal to topple Mossadegh, and it worked like a charm. Thus, Iran was prevented from receiving any revenue from its oil as a consequence of a worldwide embargo and blockade against Iranian oil which was aggressively enforced by the British Navy. Meanwhile, the US itself, in support of Britain, refused to buy Iranian oil. The result was that "the country's main source of income was gone. Iran had earned $45 million from oil exports in 1950, more than 70 percent of its total earnings. That sum dropped by half in 1951 and then to almost zero in 1952."[87]

As a May 30, 1953, "Memorandum of Conversation" between the Shah and US Ambassador Loy W. Henderson reflects, even the Shah, the US's handpicked successor to Mossadegh and soon-to-be tyrannical dictator, was alarmed at the situation.[88] As the memo relates, "Shah told by Henderson that US would not buy Iranian oil for the foreseeable future unless dispute with Britain was resolved, nor it would it give financial or economic aid." It should be noted that, as reflected in the 2017 released documents, the resolution of the oil dispute, at least on the surface, now came down to the question of how much Iran would pay Great Britain as compensation for the nationalization of the oil fields.

And, the Shah gave his opinion that the best chance for settlement was under Mossadegh rather than a successor, and he further "said that the present economic position of Iran is so dangerous that he would like to see the US give financial and economic assistance to the country even though Dr. Mossadegh was still in power and even though the extension of that assistance might make it appear that the US was supporting Mossadegh."[89]

The US was unmoved by the Shah's plea. As a later, June 19, 1953, Memorandum of Conversation relates, it was agreed by the major US decision-makers, including President Eisenhower himself, that Mossadegh would be told that the US is refusing to give him any economic aid, as "it would be unfortunate at this time to give Mossadegh any ammunition which would strengthen his political position."[90]

The US even rebuffed what appeared to be an incredible offer by Mossadegh. Thus, a May 4, 1953, Telegram from the US

Embassy in Iran to the Department of State quotes Mossadegh as stating, "I am willing have this dispute settled by someone whom Britain and I can trust. I agreeable President Eisenhower act as arbiter. I ready give him fully power to decide issue. Will you be good enough to ask President Eisenhower if he would undertake settle this matter for us?"[91] The June 19 memo relates that "it is agreed that no response should be given to Mosadeq in regard to his request that Eisenhower settle the dispute." Instead, silence would be the rude reply to Mossadegh's incredibly conciliatory proposal.[92]

While the US claimed, as it always does, that it was intervening in Iran to protect democracy and freedom, the CIA's own documents evidence a complete contempt for the will of the Iranian people and the willingness to use brutality to suppress that will. And, as time went on, the US's support for brutal repression in Iran only increased.

And so, for example, in a memo to US Ambassador Henderson, dated May 19, 1953, the counselor of Embassy, Mattison, gives his quite reasonable opinion that while forcing a change of government in Iran might lead to the US obtaining the ends it wanted, the resulting regime "would probably take the form of a military dictatorship or a dictatorship supported by the military, as there is some doubt that sufficient popular support could be obtained for a settlement on British terms."[93] History would of course prove Mattison correct in this regard.

The fact was that, as US policymakers would often acknowledge in their internal documents, Mossadegh, despite the problems he was facing—problems largely created by the conscious work of the UK and US to sink the Iranian economy—was still popular and still the single most important politician in Iran. Thus, in a May 8, 1953, Telegram from the US Embassy to the State Department, Ambassador Henderson opines that "Mosadeq still however, outstanding political figure [in] Iran."[94]

In a July 1, 1953, "Despatch from the Embassy in Iran to the Department of State," the first secretary of the Embassy actually pays tribute to Mossadegh, stating:

> There seems to be no question of the broad base of popular support for Dr. Mosadeq at the time he first took office as Prime Minister. As leader of the struggle against the Anglo-Iranian Oil Company in a country where resentment and even hatred of the British is deep-rooted, Mosadeq could count upon the support of people from all levels of society with but few exceptions. For many months after the oil nationalization, the Prime Minister's popularity continually mounted. To the common people, Mosadeq as looked upon almost as a demigod.
>
> The phenomenon of Mosadeq was almost unique in Iran. The figure of a frail, old man, in an Oriental country where age of itself commands respect, who appeared to be successfully winning a battle against remarkable odds, aroused the sympathy of all Iranians. In a country where political corruption had been the accepted norm, there now appeared a man whose patriotism and financial honesty were unassailable.[95]

Here, the Embassy paints the picture of a man of great, and indeed unique, virtue.

Again, in a July 8, 1953, memo, Kermit Roosevelt cites a trusted Iranian source, in an "estimate of Mossadegh's strength," saying the following:

> "(1) Mossadegh is the only strong political figure in Iran.
> (2) Mossadegh has the confidence of all people except a few disgruntled aristocrats.
> (3) Mossadegh cannot be ousted at this time."[96]

Given Mossadegh's popularity among the people, and still bent upon getting rid of him just the same, the CIA proceeded with its plan on forcing him out. And so, just about two weeks after the foregoing memo assessing Mossadegh's formidable strength as a political figure in Iran, the CIA, by memo dated July 22, 1953, set forth its list of around three hundred people to arrest on the night of the coup. Mossadegh was at the top of this list.[97]

Early on, as initial preparations are being made for the overthrow, the CIA lays out a list of its assets which it has had in Iran for some time, even before the coup plans had been formulated and green-lighted by Eisenhower. A March 3, 1953, CIA memo lists the following: *"Mass Propaganda means* (press, etc.): CIA controls a network with numerous press, political, and clerical contacts which has proven itself capable of disseminating large-scale . . . propaganda . . . ; *Poison Pen, personal denunciations, rumor spreading, etc.:* CIA has means of making fairly effective personal attacks against any political figure in Iran, including Mossadegh. . . . ; *Street Riots, demonstrations, mobs, etc.:* CIA [*less than 1 line not declassified*] . . . .[98] The CIA also explains that it "has one group in Iran which, it is believed, may be fairly effective in carrying on morale sabotage within the country and stimulating various types of small scale resistance."

Similarly, in but another CIA memo, dated April 16, 1953, the CIA, under a heading entitled, "Activist Assets," discusses the fact that "[less than 1 line not declassified] have the capabilities of bringing out gangs of street fighters."[99]

And, of course, the CIA had stockpiles of readily available cash and weapons. Thus, in a March 20, 1953, progress report to the National Security Council, the CIA explains that "[a]t the present the CIA has a stockpile of small arms, ammunition and demolition materiel [*less than 1 line not declassified*]. The stockpile is in quantity designed to supply a 10,000-man guerilla force for six months without resupply. . . ."[100]

As one author puts it succinctly, the CIA's "agents in Tehran bought off secular politicians, religious leaders and key military officers. They hired thugs to run rampant through the street, sometimes pretending to be Mossadegh supporters, sometimes calling for his overthrow, anything to create a chaotic political situation. Money was spread around the offices of newspaper editors and radio station owners as well."[101]

The plan was to create chaos and confusion which would be blamed on Mossadegh, and then to move against Mossadegh by arresting him at his home in the middle of the night.

The first attempt at this plan did not succeed because Mossadegh's chief of staff, General Riahi, who was marked as someone who should be arrested as well on the night of the coup and who Roosevelt then wanted killed, got wise to the plan in time and took precautions to protect Mossadegh. The coup, at this point, looked doomed, with a CIA memo dated August 17, 1953, concluding: "Except in the unlikely event that a strong and resolute opposition majority develops in some future Majilis, any future attempt to unseat Mossadegh will necessarily be an out-and-out coup, without legal sanction."[102]

However, the one thing the CIA still had going for it was the fact that few had caught on to the fact that the US had been behind the attempt. And, it would in fact be Mossadegh's faith in, and kind feelings for, the Americans that would ultimately be his undoing as we shall soon see.

As an August 16, 1953, Telegram from the US Embassy to the Department of State explains, only the communist Tudeh Party's newspaper, *Shojat*, carried any account of the attempted coup whatsoever.[103] However, Tudeh was right on the mark, explaining in the paper that "American imperialists sent [General Norman] Schwarzkopf [yes, the father of "Stormin'" Norman Schwarzkopf of First Gulf War fame] as spy to court after Dulles and Eisenhower statements with instructions present government must be ousted by military action and replaced by government headed by men like Alayar Saleh, General Zahedi, Hakimi, Dr. Amini." Luckily for the CIA, few folks of importance read the communist party paper, and so a second attempt could be made.

And, this attempt was made and succeeded in a most devious way. Thus, while Kermit Roosevelt again set plans into motion to cause street riots and other provocations, while personally hiding General Zahedi until the right moment, he needed one last ruse to pull off Operation Ajax. There is a reference to this in the CIA documents when Ambassador Henderson, in a Telegram to the US State Department, explains how he went to see Mossadegh at his home.[104] He then told the unsuspecting Mossadegh that he was "particularly concerned [about] increasing attacks on Americans," and how every hour or two he was "receiving additional reports [of] attacks on American citizens not only in Tehran but also other localities." He pleaded with Mossadegh to call on law enforcement agencies to take affirmative action to protect Americans.

What is not said here is that Henderson was meeting with Mossadegh as part of Roosevelt's plans to create enough pressure for the lid to be blown off the situation on the streets of Tehran. The problem, as Stephen Kinzer explains so well in his great book, *All The Shah's Men*, was that Mossadegh was too restrained in the face of the terrible violence being stoked by the CIA. As he relates:

> The riots that shook Tehran on Monday intensified on Tuesday. Thousands of demonstrators, unwittingly under CIA control, surged through the streets, looting shops, destroying pictures of the Shah, and ransacking the offices of royalist groups. Exuberant nationalists and communists joined in the mayhem. The police were still under orders from Mossadegh not to interfere. That allowed rioters to do their jobs, which was to give the

impression that Iran was sliding towards anarchy. Roosevelt caught glimpses of them during his furtive trips around the city and said that they 'scared the hell out of him.'

The riots were working to a point, but now Roosevelt needed an overreaction by Mossadegh to justify what amounted to a military coup in the name of restoring order and democracy. This is where Ambassador Henderson comes in. Thus, as Kinzer explains, Henderson was told by Roosevelt to go to Mossadegh and to ask him for the police to crack down on the rioters in Tehran in order to protect the lives of Americans who were allegedly under threat and attack.

In so doing, Roosevelt and Henderson were appealing to Mossadegh's better angels to undo him. As Kinzer puts it, "Roosevelt had perfectly analyzed his adversary's psyche. Mossadegh, steeped in a culture of courtliness and hospitality, found it shocking that guests in Iran were being mistreated. That shock overwhelmed his good judgment, and with Henderson still in the room, he picked up a telephone and called his police chief. Trouble in the streets had become intolerable, he said, and it was time for the police to put an end to it. With this order, Mossadegh sent the police out to attack a mob that included many of his own most fervent supporters."

The fuse had been lit, and Roosevelt was ecstatic. As he wrote in a Telegram From the Station in Iran to the Central Intelligence Agency, dated August 19, 1953, "Overthrow of Mossadegh appears on verge of success. Zahedi now at radio station."[105] By August 20, 1953, the coup had been successful, with Mossadegh's home being stormed and looted, and with Mossadegh taken away under arrest.[106] The Shah was then summoned back from his own self-imposed exile at the time prescribed by Kermit Roosevelt.

As planned, the Shah's monarchy was fully restored and General Zahedi was installed as prime minister in Mossadegh's stead. The coup government now installed, though still precari-ously, any pretenses to such lofty goals as democracy and freedom were quickly abandoned. First of all, though one might believe that the CIA's work was done, it had in fact had just begun, with the directorate of Plans for the CIA explaining in an August 1953 memo that the coup had "created a favorable atmosphere for CIA operations in the country."[107]

In a Monthly Report Prepared in the Directorate of Plans, CIA, dated September 1953, it is mentioned how General Zahedi's government was now firmly established in light of $45 million in emergency funds sent to him by the US.[108] Meanwhile, the CIA relates how the "Shah feels that the Majlis should not be brought into session because a strong authoritarian government is neces-sary to provide the country's internal stability." Further, "[t]he Shah . . . has issued orders that Mossadegh be killed immediately by his guards in case of any serious Tudeh rebellion."

Events continued to move quickly toward a more repressive system in Iran, and seemingly with US approval. For example, in a Despatch dated November 13, 1953, Roosevelt speaks openly about how he had counseled the new government that if it cannot figure out a way to change the ballot boxes [for the election for the Majili], they may play safe and just stuff them."[109] He then describes how the Shah did in fact rig the elections for Majili in a number of areas by ballot stuffing.

An Editorial Note in the newly released documents states: "[i]n a memorandum to Secretary of State Dulles, July 30, 1954, Acting Special Assistant for Intelligence Fisher Howe discussed the political prospects for Iran. He wrote that political power in Iran was exercised by the Shah and the landowning classes. . . . Iran's power structure was maintained by the continuance of martial law, the enforcement of strict press censorship, the work of the security forces, the provision of US emergency aid, and the expectation of an oil settlement in favor of Iran."[110] Similarly, a

National Intelligence Estimate dated, December 7, 1954, explains that "[t]he principal new features of the present power situation are: (a) the extensive use of authoritarian means—martial law, censorship, and prosecution or repression of opponents—to curtail opposition to the regime and the government . . . ." The Estimate goes on to state that "[s]o long as Zahedi is Prime Minister, the government will almost certainly continue a fairly firm policy of repression."[111]

Again, there is no hint here that the coup government had any plans on democratizing Iran, or that the US had any such intentions either.

Meanwhile, in a November 5, 1953, Despatch from the US Embassy to the US State Department, we see the logical result of the US collaboration with Nazi sympathizers. Thus, the Embassy, again without any apparent concern, explains that "The Shah and his administration are encouraging the growth of quasi-military and fascist-type groups as added insurance against the possibility of further Tudeh mob actions."[112]

Under the heading "Anti-Tudeh Organizations," the Embassy explains, "These organizations . . . have all the trappings of a falange or fascist type of group, even to their black-shirted uniforms. The Sumka demonstrated its strength and discipline on the occasion of the recent Sports Festival, when approximately 500 of its members impressed the crowds at the Stadium with a show of swastika-bedecked banners carried in perfect marching order. These organizations . . . almost certainly receive their excellent financial backing from the Shah and the administration."

Meanwhile, the UK and the US both got what they wanted all along with the fall of Mossadegh.

Thus, the Anglo-Iranian Oil Company was reorganized into British Petroleum, or BP for short.[113] And, according to an Appendix in the newly released documents, it received 40 percent of the Iranian oil industry.[114] The US received another 40 percent of the industry, split between five companies—according to the Appendix, Gulf-International Company (8 percent), Standard Oil Company of California (now, Chevron) (8 percent), Standard Oil of New Jersey (now, ExxonMobil) (8 percent), Texas Company (now, a subsidiary of Chevron) (8 percent), and Socony-Vacuum Overseas Supply Company (now, ExxonMobil) (8 percent). An additional 14 percent of Iran's industry went to Royal Dutch Shell, with the remaining 4 percent to a French company.

For his grand prize, Kermit Roosevelt would become vice president of Gulf Oil, a quite natural next job for the man who helped make Iran safe for Western oil companies, including Gulf itself. To his credit, though, he left the CIA for a job at Gulf because, while forever proud of his coup orchestration in Iran, he was not interested in going along with the Dulles Brothers next coup in Guatemala in 1954.[115] Roosevelt was rightly fearful that the CIA would get too used to overthrowing foreign governments, many times against the will of the people, and he did not believe that was a prudent or ethical idea.[116]

For many Iranians, the nature of the Shah's reign is best typified by his infamous security apparatus known as the SAVAK. The nature of the SAVAK, moreover, says much about the nature of the foreign policy of the United States which helped to create it and support it for over twenty years.

A great, succinct summary of the SAVAK, and the US relationship with it, can be found in Dean Henderson's *Big Oil and Their Bankers in the Persian Gulf*:

> By 1957 the Company, as intelligence insiders know the CIA, created one of its first Frankensteins—the Shah of Iran's brutal secret police known as SAVAK. . . .
>
> Three hundred fifty SAVAK agents were shuttled each year to CIA training facilities in McLean, Virginia, where they learned the finer arts of interrogation and torture. . . .

From 1957–79 Iran housed 125,000 political prisoners. SAVAK "disappeared" dissenters, a strategy replicated by CIA surrogate dictators in Argentina and Chile.

. . . In 1974 the director of Amnesty International declared that no country had a worse human rights record than Iran. The CIA responded by increasing its support for SAVAK.[117]

For its part, the *Washington Post*, in an article written shortly after the Islamic Revolution, acknowledges that "the CIA 'definitely' trained SAVAK agents in 'both physical and psychological' torture techniques . . . ."[118] The article explained that there were "'[j]oint activities'" between the SAVAK and the CIA and Israel's Mossad, and that "[t]he Israelis even wrote SAVAK's manuals . . . ."

Well-trained by the CIA, the "Savak—*Sazman-i Etelaat va Amniyat-I Keshvar*, the 'National Information and Security Organization'—was to become the most notorious and murderous [of the Shah's security services], its torture chambers among the Middle's East's most terrible institutions."[119]

The SAVAK was the original incubator used by the CIA to develop its torture techniques for worldwide distribution. One grisly example of this was illustrated by Mohamed Heikal, one of the "greatest Egyptian journalists, . . . [who] described how Savak filmed the torture of a young Iranian woman, how she was stripped naked and how cigarettes were then used to burn her nipples. According to Heikal, the film was later distributed by the CIA to other intelligence agencies working for American-supported regimes around the world including Taiwan, Indonesia and the Philippines."

The techniques used by the SAVAK, many borrowed from the Nazis and then passed along to the SAVAK by the CIA,[120] were uniquely grisly and terrible. And, the SAVAK operated much like the Gestapo, entering a person's home at night, hauling the person away, and many times disappearing that person forever.

As Robert Fisk explains, "[t]he Shah was finally persuaded to allow the International Committee of the Red Cross into Iran's prisons in 1977; they were allowed to see more than 3,000 'security detainees'—political prisoners—in eighteen different jails. They recorded that the inmates had been beaten, burned with cigarettes and chemicals, tortured with electrodes, raped, sodomized with bottles and boiling eggs. Interrogators forced electric cables into the uterus of female prisoners. The Red Cross report named 124 prisoners who had died under torture."

The first comprehensive report I could find from Amnesty International on Iran and the SAVAK was a briefing dated November 1976—just as Jimmy "Human Rights" Carter was preparing to take office as president. The Amnesty International Briefing, Iran, November 1976[121] makes for fascinating, if not horrifying, reading, and gives one a glimpse into the dark world which the US played a key role in manufacturing for the Iranian people.

Amnesty International (AI) described Iran as "in theory a constitutional monarchy with a partially elected parliament, but in practice the Shah has supreme authority."[122] As AI explained, "[o]ne important instrument of the Shah's authority is the army . . . [and] [t]he other, equally important, is the National Intelligence and Security Organization (SAVAK) which was formed in 1957 'for the purposes of security of the country and prevention of any kind of conspiracy detrimental to public interests . . . .' The head of the SAVAK is appointed by the Shah and wields unlimited power."

AI related that "[t]he suppression of political opposition is carried out by SAVAK with extreme ruthlessness using a system of informers which permeates all levels of Iranian society and which has created an atmosphere of fear remarked on by visitors to Iran and emphasized by opponents of the regime outside the country."[123]

Torture was endemic, and indeed central, to the Shah's reign. As AI reported, "[a]ll observers to trials since 1965 have reported allegations of torture . . . . Alleged methods of torture include whipping and beating, electric shocks, the extraction of nails and teeth, boiling water pumped into the rectum, heavy weights hung on the testicles, tying the prisoner to a metal table heated to white heat, inserting a broken bottle into the anus, and rape."

The very existence of the SAVAK belies any claims that the US somehow cares about human rights, democracy, or freedom, or that it wants such things for the Iranian people. And certainly, the Iranian people must be forgiven if they do not believe that the US has their best interests at heart.

Iranians have every reason and right to feel anger and even hatred toward the United States, not just for what the US has done to them, but also because the US continues to do so while holding itself out as a bright beacon of democracy and freedom in the world. The US's as pretense of being a uniquely righteous country must be hard to bear for many in the world, not just the Iranians.

Moreover, as we would see time and again, the US's meddling in another country would be followed by meddling in our own democratic processes. Thus, Ronald Reagan would exploit the hostage-taking which followed the Iranians' revolution against the US-backed Shah in 1979 to steal the 1980 presidential elections in the US.

As intrepid journalist Robert Parry helped to expose, Reagan worked with senior Republicans, including George H.W. Bush (former CIA director and then Reagan's running mate), high-level CIA officers not appointed by Carter, and Israeli intelligence as used long-time assets in Tehran—assets which both the United States and Israel had cultivated for years under the Shah—to prevail upon the hostage takers to hold the American hostages at the former US Embassy longer in order to undermine

Carter's chances at reelection. As Parry writes, "[t]he idea was that by persuading the Iranians to hold the 52 American hostages until after the US presidential election, Carter would be made to look weak and inept, essentially dooming his hopes for a second term."[124]

According to Parry, Israeli intelligence agent Ari Ben-Menashe, among other "October Surprise" witnesses, gave sworn testimony about the "meetings between Republicans and Iranians in 1980 that were designed with the help of CIA personnel and Israeli intelligence to delay release of the 52 hostages until after Carter's defeat."

Parry quite correctly compares this coup plot against Carter to the plot against Mossadegh himself, though, of course, the target of the coup plot in this case was a sitting American president. There is probably no better illustration of the United States' habitual overthrow of foreign governments coming back to haunt us, and our own democracy, than this event. And, it should not be surprising that the chickens would come back to roost in this way. When any individual or institution (e.g., the CIA) becomes too comfortable with making deals with devils to obtain such ends as regime change elsewhere, it is but one small step beyond this to making such deals to implement regime change at home. In this way, the CIA and its immoral coup plotting has become a grave danger to our own Republic.

4

GUATEMALA

THE NEXT COUNTRY ON THE CIA chopping block was Guatemala whose crime was to have a revolution in 1944 which overthrew a military dictatorship, established democratic rule, and gave land and a modicum of dignity to its mostly peasant population. As Noam Chomsky, quoting a CIA memorandum from 1952, describes:

> Furthermore, the 1944 revolution had aroused "a strong national movement to free Guatemala from the military dictatorship, social backwardness, and 'economic colonialism' which had been the pattern of the past," and "inspired the loyalty and conformed to the self-interest of most politically conscious Guatemalans." Things became still worse after a successful land reform began to threaten "stability" in neighboring countries where suffering people did not fail to take notice.
>
> In short, the situation was pretty awful.[125]

In light of the above, and the fact that some of the land reform was to come at the expense of United Fruit Company (now Chiquita) whose land the government was willing to purchase at the market rate, the Guatemala government, led by President

Jacobo Arbenz, was deemed a "Communist threat" which had to be overthrown.[126]

A good glimpse into the US-orchestrated coup which followed can be found in the now-declassified report of the CIA's own historian, Nicholas Cullather, whose candor is quite refreshing. As Cullather explains:

> The CIA's operation to overthrow the Government of Guatemala in 1954 marked an early zenith in the Agency's long record of covert action. Following closely on the successful operations that installed the Shah as ruler of Iran [redacted] the Guatemalan operation, known as PBSUCCESS, was both more ambitious and more thoroughly successful than either precedent. Rather than helping a prominent contender gain power with a few inducements, PBSUCCESS used an intensive paramilitary and psychological campaign to replace a popular, elected government with a political non-entity.[127]

This operation clearly proved the old adage that "there's no success like failure," for from the point of view of promoting democracy, freedom, and development, this was a grandiose failure.

As Cullather himself concedes, ""[t]he overthrown Arbenz government was not, [as] many contend, a Communist regime but a reformist government that offered perhaps the last chance for progressive, democratic change in the region." This is a heartbreaking epitaph on the CIA's "successful" operation, and the situation became far worse as time went on.

Cullather describes how United Fruit, one of the prime movers behind the coup, became oppositional toward Arbenz shortly after his inauguration in March of 1951, and before Arbenz began his land reform policy and the confiscation of lands which followed. Thus, United Fruit expressed concern over the potential of increased labor costs under Arbenz in August of 1951, warning its "employees that any increase in labor costs would make its operations in Guatemala uneconomic and force it to withdraw from the country."

In September, United Fruit then suspended 3,742 employees at its Tiquisate banana plantation, but was later ordered by the labor court of appeals to reinstate them with back pay. Meanwhile, United Fruit gave an ultimatum to Arbenz that it would not restart its plantations "without assurance of stable labor costs for three years and exemption from unfavorable labor laws and exchange controls."

President Arbenz then enacted the Agrarian Reform Law on June 17, 1952. Almost immediately thereafter, on July 10, 1952, Allen Dulles, the director of the CIA, went to "solicit State Department approval for plan to overthrow Arbenz."[128] This approval was not hard in coming given that Allen's brother, John Foster Dulles, was the secretary of State.

Moreover, as David Talbot explains, United Fruit had key connections all over Washington, D.C.:

> But United Fruit had no more powerful friends in the adminis-
> tration than the Dulles brothers.
>
> The Dulles' had served as United Fruit's lawyers from their
> earliest days at Sullivan and Cromwell. On the eve of World War
> I, young [John] Foster made a discreet tour of Central America
> on behalf of United Fruit, which was growing concerned about
> labor unrest and creeping Bolshevism in its tropical empire. . . .
>
> Allen became so frequent a visitor to Guatemala as a legal
> envoy for United Fruit that he began taking along [his wife]
> Clover, who fell under the spell of the country's beauty and
> culture. . . . But the Dulles' interest in Guatemalan artifacts did
> not extend to the people who had produced them.[129]

On February 25, 1953, Guatemala confiscated 234,000 acres of land owned by United Fruit, and this appeared to be the last straw, for the National Security Council authorized covert action against Guatemala in short order.[130] However, it must be noted that the land confiscated, as required by Arbenz's land reform law, was unused land. As Eduardo Galeano explains, this land reform law had benefited "over 100,000 families, although the law only affected idle lands and paid expropriated owners an ind emnity in bonds.[131] But since United Fruit was using a mere 8 percent of its land, which extended from ocean to ocean, its unused lands began to be distributed to the peasants."[132]

Meanwhile, by the end of 1953, CIA Director Allen Dulles allocated $3 million for the overthrow of Arbenz. That would amount to over $27 million in today's dollars. And, because there was no real Soviet threat in Guatemala, the US had to manufacture one. And so, in February of 1954, the CIA began Operation WASHTUB, "a plan to plant phony Soviet arms cache . . . ." As for the alleged Soviet threat, the CIA would locate and go through one hundred fifty thousand documents recovered in Guatemala after the coup to try to find any evidence thereof. It found no such evidence.

Meanwhile, to carry out the coup, the CIA trained and led paramilitary forces to invade and carry out sabotage operations in Guatemala. This was combined with a US Navy blockade of Guatemala; radio broadcasts which spread anti-Arbenz propaganda; CIA plane overflights and strafing of troop trains; and bombings by F-14s. All of this combined to force Arbenz to resign and to ultimately go into exile.

The aftermath for Guatemala was simply disastrous, as the CIA's own historian admits. Thus, the fallout was multifold. Writing in 1994, Cullather explains, "Castillo Armas's new regime proved embarrassingly inept. Its repressive and corrupt policies soon polarized Guatemala and provoked renewed civil conflict. Operation PBSUCCESS aroused resentments that continue, almost 40 years after the event, to prevent the Agency from revealing its role."

Cullather further relates that, following Arbenz's removal from office, thousands of peasants who insisted staying on the land given to them under the agrarian reform law were arrested.

Furthermore, while the US claimed to have saved Guatemala from the boot of oppression, that boot was in fact about to fall heavily on the Guatemalan people. Thus, Castillo Armas named José Bernabé Linares "to head the new regime's security forces." Significantly, Linares had been "the hated secret police chief" of Guatemala's former strongman and US ally, Jorge Ubico—the Nazi sympathizer who was overthrown in the revolution of 1944. And, Linares would quickly take actions that resembled those of Nazis, banning "all 'subversive' literature, including works by Victor Hugo and Fyodor Dostoevsky."

For his part, "Castillo Armas completed his lunge to the right by disenfranchising illiterates (two-thirds of the electorate); canceling land reform, and outlawing all political parties, labor confederations, and peasant organizations. Finally, he decreed a 'political statute' that voided the 1945 constitution and gave him complete executive and legislative authority."

And things went from bad to worse from there. Thus, Castillo Armas himself was assassinated by a member of his own presidential guard, and Guatemala slid into chaos, civil war, and rule by successive military regimes. As Cullather laments, "in 1966, the United States responded by sending military advisers and weapons [on the side of the military junta to fight a growing insurgency by the peasants], escalating a cycle of violence and reprisals that by the end of the decade claimed the lives of a US Ambassador, two US military attaches, and as many as 10,000 peasants."

Another, and unintended, consequence of the Guatemalan operation, according to Cullather, was that it taught revolutionaries like Fidel Castro that there was not a peaceful path to social change in Latin America in light of the US's willingness itself to use force to suppress such change. They learned that revolution was only possible through the barrel of a gun, and that the gun must be turned quickly against the foes of the revolution once it succeeded.

An interesting historical note here is that, according to E. Howard Hunt, a CIA spook who was part of the coup against Arbenz, he allowed a number of revolutionaries who were captured during the coup to go free as he was about to board a plane home to the US.[133] One of these revolutionaries, standing on the runway as his plane took off, was none other than Ernesto Guevara, who would soon be known to the world simply as Che. As history would show, Che really took the foregoing lessons of the Guatemalan coup to heart.

And, while Hunt would later regret letting Guevara go, he would ultimately get his man, playing a key role in tracking Che down in Bolivia, and making possible his capture and murder in 1967.[134] It is also important to note that Che's ultimate capture and murder were made possible by the CIA's buying the 1966 Bolivian elections. As William Blum explains, "[t]he CIA bestowed $600,000 upon President René Barrientos and lesser sums to several right-wing parties in a successful effort to influence the outcome of national elections. Gulf Oil contributed two hundred thousand more to Barrientos."[135] It was Barrientos' armed forces, closely allied with and directed by the CIA, who would ultimately determine Che's fate.

Meanwhile, Cullather concludes that "[i]n Guatemala, US officials learned a lesson they would relearn in Vietnam, Iran, [redacted] and other countries: Intervention usually produces 'allies' that are stubborn, aid hungry, and corrupt." But in truth, as should be quite evident to even the casual observer, US officials have never truly learned that lesson, and they continue to aggressively intervene in other countries around the world with equally disastrous results.

Meanwhile, the grisly violence in Guatemala continued to spin out of control with the US's connivance. In 1981, just as Ronald Reagan was taking office, Amnesty International put out a huge report entitled, "Guatemala, A government program of political murder," which detailed the abuses of the post-Arbenz Guatemalan dictatorship and its paramilitary death squads. As Amnesty International related:

> The human rights issue that dominates all others in the Republic of Guatemala is that people who oppose or are imagined to oppose the government are systematically seized without warrant, tortured and murdered, and that these tortures and murders are part of a deliberate and long-standing program of the Guatemalan government.
>
> This report contains information, published for the first time, which shows how the selection of targets for detention and murder, and the deployment of official forces for extralegal operations, can be pin-pointed to secret offices [of the G-2 death squads] in an annex of Guatemala's National Palace, under the direct control of the President of the Republic. . . .
>
> Between January and November in 1980 alone some 3,000 people described by government representatives as 'subversives' and 'criminals' were either shot on the spot in political assassination or seized and murdered later; at least 364 others seized have not yet been accounted for.[136]

As Amnesty International further related, "[p]olitical killings and 'disappearances' involving government forces are not new in Guatemala. In 1976 Amnesty International estimated that about 20,000 people had been victims of these abuses since 1966, when they first began to occur regularly." Of course, it was in 1966 that the US began its period of military intervention on the side of the Guatemalan government against a popular insurgency. It is no coincidence that that is also when the mass slaughter of Guatemalans began, for the US was a key part of Guatemala's killing machine.

The well-respected journalist Allan Nairn, writing in 1995, explained that one hundred ten thousand Guatemalans had been murdered since 1978 by CIA-backed death squads.[137] As Nairn related:

> North American CIA operatives work inside a Guatemalan Army unit that maintains a network of torture centers and has killed thousands of Guatemalan civilians. The G-2, headquartered on the fourth floor of the Guatemalan National Palace has, since at least the 1960s, been advised, trained, armed and equipped by US undercover agents. Working out of the US Embassy and living in safehouses and hotels, these agents work through an elite group of Guatemalan officers who are secretly paid by the CIA and who have been implicated personally in numerous political crimes and assassinations.

Nairn relates that "[a]t least three of the recent G-2 chiefs have been paid by the CIA, according to US and Guatemalan intelligence services." One of these death squad chiefs, Otto Perez Molina, would become Guatemalan president in 2012. As Nairn explains, "these men are only cogs in a large US government apparatus. Colonel Hooker, the former DIA chief for Guatemala, says, '[i]t would be an embarrassing situation if you ever had a roll call of everybody in the Guatemalan Army who ever collected a CIA paycheck.' Hooker says the agency payroll is so large it encompasses most of the army's top-decision makers."

All told, around 200,000 civilians were killed during the civil conflict which lasted from 1962 to 1996.[138] Guatemala's 1999 truth commission "estimated that the army was responsible for

93 percent of the killings and leftist guerrillas for three percent. Four percent were listed as unresolved."[139] That is, the US-backed Guatemalan military was responsible for nearly all of these killings. Meanwhile, most of the victims were Mayan Indian. It is now generally recognized, in fact, that this slaughter of the Mayan Indians constituted genocide.

Trade union leaders were also murdered in large numbers during these years in Guatemala. As a union lawyer myself who has been involved in challenging the repression of fellow trade unionists in Latin America, I had the occasion to visit the site of one of the more notorious string of killings of union leaders, and to hear from some of the survivors. In the late 1970s, eight union leaders at a Coca-Cola plant in Guatemala City were murdered in short order, including two successive local union presidents. I visited their local union hall which to this day memorializes those killed during this period in colorful wall paintings.

As the *New York Times* reported, those unionists who survived "believe at least some of the assaults have been carried out by policemen and soldiers acting under official orders . . . ."[140] They also believed that the local owner of the bottling plant was the driving force behind these murders. The same article reported that, on one occasion, "Coca-Cola organizers were present at a meeting of 27 Guatemalan labor leaders that was broken up by armed men. All 27 were taken away, and none was heard from again." This type of event was common under dictatorial rule in Guatemala.

The most intense years of the killings, however, took place under the dictatorship of Gen Efrain Rios Montt which lasted from 1982 to 1983. Montt, in turn, was backed to the hilt by President Ronald Reagan who lionized Montt. Montt personally "ordered the main highland massacres (662 villages destroyed, by the army's own count) . . . ."[141] Robert Parry describes the

cruel way in which Guatemalan armed forces operated during
this period:

> On March 17, 1983, Americas Watch condemned the
> Guatemalan army for human rights atrocities against the
> Indian population.
>
> New York attorney Stephen L. Kass said these findings
> included proof that the government carried out 'virtually
> indiscriminate murder of men, women and children of any
> farm regarded by the army as possibly supportive of guerrilla
> insurgents.'
>
> Rural women suspected of guerrilla sympathies were raped
> before execution, Kass said, adding that children were 'thrown
> into burning homes. They are thrown in the air and speared
> with bayonets. We heard many, many stories of children being
> picked up by the ankles and swung against poles so their heads
> are destroyed.'[142]

The Reagan White House and the CIA were well aware of
the terrible violence that Montt was carrying out, but Reagan
nonetheless increased military aid to his regime, and prevailed
upon Israel to provide additional military assistance of the type
which was politically inexpedient for his administration to provide—namely, military helicopters used in firing at villages from
the air.[143]

Still, a number of US presidents, from Eisenhower to
Clinton, had their fingerprints on this genocidal killing spree. As
Nairn relates, the CIA operations in support of the death squads
are part of the larger US policy. The Bush and Clinton State
Departments, for example, in the midst of a much-touted 'cutoff'
of military aid to Guatemala after 1990, authorized—according
to classified State Department records—more than 114 separate
sales of US pistols and rifles.

The killing of defenseless people has been state policy in Guatemala for thirty years. The question is not whether the US government has known it—it is obviously aware of its own actions. It is why, with overt and covert aid, it has helped commit the army's murders.

The sad truth, moreover, is that the violence and murders, particularly aimed at the Mayan peoples, did not end with the official cessation of the civil war in 1996. As one commentator explains: "[t]he conflict was underpinned by poverty, marginalization and racism against Mayan indigenous people, all of which still persist today—sometimes with violent consequences."[144] Thus, indigenous community leaders continue to be jailed, many times without trial, and even killed in significant numbers. An August 9, 2018, story explains that "[e]leven Human Rights activists and social leaders have been killed between May and July [2018] in Guatemala; U.N. experts have called for an independent investigation into the matter and for the State to consider making a greater attempt to protect them. The murdered activists were mainly indigenous people fighting against corporations and in defense of their land rights according to the statement."[145]

In short, the US's meddling in Guatemala in 1954 opened a Pandora's Box of horribles for the Guatemalan people, and the more the US meddled over the years, the worse things got for them. And, there is no prospect that what has been broken in Guatemala, including the peace and the Mayan culture and language, will ever be repaired. This indeed was a case of meddling of the most profound and evil kind.

5

CONGO & THE MOST IMPORTANT ASSASSINATION OF THE TWENTIETH CENTURY

GEORGES NZONGOLA-NTALAJA, WRITING FOR *THE GUARDIAN* of London, called it "the most important assassination of the twentieth century."[146] He was referring to the murder of the first legally elected prime minister of the Democratic Republic of the Congo ("DRC" or "Congo"), Patrice Lumumba, on January 17, 1961, through the combined efforts of the United States and Belgium. The assassination took place less than seven months after Congolese independence from Belgium. Congo has yet to recover from this tragic event.

Congo has been brutalized by the West for centuries. Of course, from the early 1500s to 1860, millions of Congolese were forcibly taken from their land and sold as slaves, first in Europe and then in the "New World." Even by 1526, the country, then a kingdom, was becoming devastated by the slave trade. As Congo's king, Nzinga Mbemba Alffonso, wrote at this time, "'Each day the traders are kidnapping our people—children of this country, sons of our nobles and vassals, even people of our own family. . . . This corruption are depravity are so widespread that our land is entirely depopulated.'"[147] At the time, Congo's children were being shipped to Europe.

Then, from 1650 to 1860, approximately three million slaves were carried across the "dreaded passage" from Congo (along with what is now Angola) to the Americas.[148] As Adam Hochschild notes in his classic, *King Leopold's Ghost*, "[r]oughly one of every four slaves imported to work the cotton and tobacco plantations of the American South began his or her journey across the Atlantic from equatorial Africa, including the Kongo Kingdom."[149] And sadly, the enslavement of the Congolese did not end with the cessation of the TransAtlantic slave trade. To the contrary, it was just about to begin on a much larger scale.

Thus, in the early 1880s, King Leopold II of Belgium, with the crucial help of explorer and mapper Henry Morton Stanley—the Welsh American of "Stanley and Livingstone" fame who curiously was a veteran of both sides of the US Civil War—personally took control and dominion over the Congo. Leopold did so on the pretext of humanitarian purposes through his International Association of the Congo, which he likened to the Red Cross and which he claimed would bring progress to the free peoples of the region and protect them from Arab slave traders.[150] In reality, the goal was the direct opposite.

Through Stanley's successful lobbying efforts, the United States was the very first country to recognize King Leopold's claim to the Congo in 1884, with the US secretary of State declaring, "[t]he Government of the United States announces its sympathy with and approval of the humane and benevolent purposes of the International Association of the Congo, administering, as it does the interest of the Free States there established . . . ."[151] This recognition, Stanley wrote, "'was the birth unto new life of the Association.'" This was also the birth of "humanitarian interventionism," as it is known today—the fantastic doctrine pursuant to which the West, and especially the US, forcibly spreads disaster and chaos throughout the world in the name of human rights and freedom.

Receiving support from humanitarians and philanthropists around the globe, including those attending Leopold's

Anti-Slavery Conference in Brussels, and aided by Christian missionaries who helped raise stolen Congolese children to serve in his armies, Leopold terrorized, enslaved, starved, mutilated (most famously by cutting off their hands), and murdered Congolese in huge numbers in the interest of profiting from the Congo's rich rubber plantations. All told, it is estimated that, under Leopold's cruel reign, the population of Congo was cut "'by at least a half,'" from twenty million to ten million between 1890 and 1920. Leopold's ravaging of Congo was indeed on a holocaustal scale.[152]

In the early 1920s, this huge loss of life became of great concern to Belgium which then commissioned the first census of Congo, not due to concerns about the lives or well-being of Africans, but because of concerns that the labor force so desperately needed for rubber output was becoming rapidly depleted.[153] It turns out that cruelty and neglect, while fine to a point, were surprisingly bad for business when taken to extremes.

Ultimately, Leopold's scheme was outed by the Congo Reform Association, and most notably by one of the leaders of its US branch, Mark Twain, whose honest and revelatory writings about Leopold in Congo shocked the world, and especially Leopold's benevolent benefactors. This ultimately led to Belgium taking Congo out of Leopold's hands and to Belgium's administering it as a traditional European colony. As Hochschild laments, however, while the worst excesses of Leopold ended at this point, the Congolese continued to be forced into labor and chewed up in the rubber plantation system that Leopold created.[154] And, their exploitation only increased after WWI with the discovery of rich copper, gold, tin, and uranium deposits which the Congolese were then forced to mine in terrible, backbreaking conditions.

Relief at least appeared in sight in 1960 when the people of the Congo won their independence from Belgium and elected their first president, Joseph Kasavubu, and their first prime minister,

Patrice Lumumba. However, the hope for an independent Congo would be short-lived.

As Ludo De Witte explains in his groundbreaking book, *The Assassination of Lumumba*, after WWII, countries throughout the Third World began to throw off their colonial shackles. And 1960 was a year in which Africa rose up to claim its independence. As De Witte writes, "[t]he UN declared 1960 the year of Africa; no less than sixteen states on the black continent gained their independence that year, and the largest and potentially richest of them was the Congo."[155]

The West, led by the US which was desirous of replacing Europe as the world's great neo-colonial power, was not thrilled by these independence movements in Africa. And so, a concerted effort was made by the Western powers to at least bend these movements in a direction which favored their interests. As De Witte explains, "Lumumba barred the way to this goal, because he advocated a complete decolonization that would benefit the population as a whole. He had, therefore, to be stopped."[156]

Despite the country's formal independence from Belgium, white Belgians continued to command the Congolese armed forces. According to De Witte, "Brussels's trump card in controlling Lumumba's government was the Congolese army's Belgian officer corps," which "was a legacy of the colonial army," and which "had developed an extremely conservative caste mentality . . . ."[157] The Congolese armed forces, understandably upset by this incongruent state of affairs as well as their poor pay and treatment, quickly mutinied against their Belgian commanders and in some instances turned their wrath against Belgian settlers. In response, more Belgian military forces were sent in to protect their interests.

Meanwhile, UN mission forces were also sent in, ostensibly to keep peace. However, these forces were fully under the control of the US which was "the[ir] major financier and political supporter . . . ,"[158] and they ultimately assisted the US and Belgium in undermining and then overthrowing Lumumba.[159] Moreover, while the UN forces were to replace the Belgian forces, the latter refused to leave.[160] To make matters worse, the Belgians actually helped lead a secessionist movement in the province of Katanga which precipitated the destabilization of the new central government.[161] It was in this context that Lumumba was brought down.

In his *Guardian* article, Nzongola-Ntalaja explains that Lumumba's murder—"the country's original sin"—was motivated by the US's desire to control the Congo's resources. Indeed, as he relates, the US had begun to intervene in Congo even before independence:

> When the atrocities related to brutal economic exploitation in Leopold's Congo Free State resulted in millions of fatalities, the US joined other world powers to force Belgium to take over the country as a regular colony. And it was during the colonial period that the US acquired a strategic stake in the enormous natural wealth of the Congo, following its use of the uranium from Congolese mines to manufacture the first atomic weapons, the Hiroshima and Nagasaki bombs.
>
> With the outbreak of the Cold War, it was inevitable that the US and its western allies would not be prepared to let Africans have effective control over strategic raw materials, lest these fall in the hands of their enemies in the Soviet camp. It is in this regard that Patrice Lumumba's determination to achieve genuine independence and to have full control over Congo's resources in order to utilize them to improve the living conditions of our people was perceived as a threat to western interests.

The US State Department has also admitted that the US intervened before independence to try to prevent Lumumba from being elected in the first place. As its Office of the Historian explains, "Even before Congolese independence, the US Government attempted to ensure election of a pro-Western government by identifying and supporting individual pro-US leaders."[162] (It is interesting to note, in light of this admission, that the Oxford University study of US/Russia election meddling lists the 1960 Congo presidential elections as one in which the USSR meddled, but not the US.)

The attempts to keep Lumumba out of power were based on claims of some in the Eisenhower administration that he was a Communist under undue influence of the Soviets—assessments which former US officials who knew Lumumba at the time later admitted were mistaken.[163] Based upon these mistaken claims, however, the CIA would embark on its largest covert operation in its history up to that time.[164]

Thus, when US machinations failed to prevent Lumumba's election, the US quickly turned to other means. According to the Office of the Historian of the US State Department:

> In August 1960, the US Government launched a covert political program in the Congo lasting almost 7 years, initially aimed at eliminating Lumumba from power and replacing him with a more moderate, pro-Western leader. The US Government provided advice and financial subsidies.[165]

To put a finer point on it, "Richard Bessell, the CIA's Deputy Director for Plans and its head of clandestine operations, said later: 'The Agency had put a top priority, probably, on a range of different methods of getting rid of Lumumba in the sense of either destroying him physically, incapacitating him, or eliminating his political influence.'"[166]

The US covert program against Lumumba included "organizing mass demonstrations, distributing anti-Communist pamphlets, and providing propaganda material for broadcasts."[167]

But this was just the tip of the iceberg. Again, according to the State Department's Office of the Historian:

> Based on authorization from President Eisenhower's statements at an NSC meeting on August 18, 1960, discussions began to develop highly sensitive, tightly-held plans to assassinate Lumumba. After Lumumba's death at the hands of Congolese rivals in January 1961, the US Government authorized the provision of paramilitary and air support to the new Congolese Government.[168]

As for the assassination efforts, there is no question that the CIA initially made plans to poison Lumumba, with the CIA's top scientist transporting the poison to Congo where it was to be placed in Lumumba's food or toothpaste.[169] This plot was made pursuant the orders of "Director of Central Intelligence Allen Dulles [who] cabled the Leopoldville Station Chief that there was agreement in 'high quarters' that Lumumba's removal must be an urgent and prime objective."[170] While the plan to poison Lumumba ended up being abandoned, the assassination plot did not end there. Thus, the US was able to carry out its plans to eliminate Lumumba through its chief asset in Congo—Joseph Mobutu—as well as through the US's Belgian allies.

As Stephen R. Weissman, who has written extensively on the CIA operation against Lumumba, explains:

> Covert CIA actions against the Lumumba government, often dovetailing with Belgian ones, culminated in Colonel Joseph Mobutu's military coup, which was 'arranged and supported and indeed managed' by the CIA alone, according to [CIA Station Chief Larry] Devlin's private interview with the [Senator Frank] Church Committee staff.

The CIA station and US embassy provided their inexperienced and politically weak Congolese protégés with a steady stream of political and military recommendations. . . . Devlin's counsel was largely heeded on critical matters, especially when it came to Lumumba. Thus Mobutu and former president Joseph Kasavubu were persuaded to resist political pressures to reconcile with Lumumba, and Mobutu reluctantly acceded to Devlin's request to arrest him.[171]

And then Devlin assented to Lumumba's being moved from the capital (then called Leopoldville after the Belgian King) by Mobutu to his "'sworn enemy" in Katanga where, Mobutu made it clear, he "'might be executed.'"[172] At this time, Katanga was under the firm control of Belgian-backed separatists. Devlin not only assented to the transfer to Katanga, but he held off telling the US State Department for three days lest the State Department try to intervene to stop the execution.[173] Lumumba was, within those three days, murdered by Congolese secessionists and their Belgian backers. For good measure, the Belgians "attempted to erase all memory of Lumumba by chopping up his corpse and dissolving the butchered pieces in acid . . . ."[174]

The Congo would not never be the same. As Weissman explains, "Fifty years ago, the former Belgian Congo received its independence under the democratically elected government of former Prime Minister Patrice Lumumba. Less than seven months later, Lumumba and two colleagues were, in the contemporary idiom, 'rendered' to their Belgian-backed secessionist enemies, who tortured them before putting them before a firing squad. The Congo would not hold another democratic election for 46 years."

And indeed, the US would see to it that no such elections would be held, making sure that their man in Zaire, as it came to be known under his rule, Joseph Mobutu (later self-named Mobutu Sese Seko), remained in power with an iron hand. All told, the US gave Mobutu "well over a billion dollars in civilian and military aid during the three decades of his rule," helping him to "repel several attempts to overthrow him."[175] The State Department, in quite sober but revealing terms, puts it this way:

> Despite periodic uprisings and unrest, Mobutu ruled the Congo (renamed Zaire in 1971) until the mid-1990s. Viewed as mercurial and occasionally irrational, Mobutu nonetheless proved to be a staunch ally against Communist encroachment in Africa. As such, he received extensive US financial, matériel, and political support, which increased his stature in much of Sub-Saharan Africa where he often served the interests of administrations from Johnson through Reagan.[176]

Sadly, the US intervention in Congo did not end with Reagan or with the Mobuto regime. Rather, President Bill Clinton would intervene in even more deadly ways, finding a path to Congo through its neighbor to the east, Rwanda.

Clinton's first disastrous move for the people of this African region was to aid and abet the genocide in Rwanda in 1994. As we know now from declassified documents,[177] as well as from Dr. Gregory Stanton[178] who worked in Clinton's State Department at the time, Bill Clinton knew about genocide just as it was beginning to unfold in Rwanda; Clinton "lied" (in Stanton's words) that he did not know about it; and the Clinton administration then affirmatively acted at the UN Security Council to have UN peacekeeping troops, then on the ground, removed, at a critical moment.

As the National Security Archive at Georgetown University explains:

> By April 15, [just over a week into the genocide] the US delegation at the UN dropped a "bombshell" on the Security Council's secret deliberations, arguing for total termination of

the mission and pullout of the peacekeepers, only to find they did not have the votes given opposition from the Non-Aligned Movement and others. On April 21, the Security Council voted to reduce the force in Rwanda from over 2,000 troops down to 270, which US ambassador Madeleine Albright in an earlier cable had all-too-accurately called a "skeletal staff."

Experts and former officials gathered at The Hague last year for a critical oral history conference reviewing the Rwanda tragedy agreed that the UN pullout decision was a turning point, a "green light" for genocide, a "disastrous decision [with] horrendous consequences," as the Nigerian UN envoy Ibrahim Gambari called it.

As we know, about eight hundred thousand Rwandans lost their lives as a result of Clinton's machinations, which, according to the National Security Archives, were carried out for the pretty meager *quid pro quo* of getting the French to agree to send peace-keepers to Somalia after the "Black Hawk Down" debacle.

And, the worst bloodshed was yet to come. Paul Kagame's Tutsi forces known as the Rwandan Patriotic Front (RPF), which committed their own mass slaughter during the hundred-day genocide in 1994 as the US knew full well,[179] took power after the genocide and hold power still. Clinton hailed Kagame as a human rights hero, and he has often been portrayed as such in popular culture (e.g., in the "Hotel Rwanda") but he was anything but.

Nonetheless, Clinton would support Kagame in his invasion of Congo under the "humanitarian" pretext of going after the *genocidaires* there. In the process, Kagame's forces would commit an even greater genocide in the DRC.

As an excellent report by The World Policy Institute explains:

The Clinton administration attempted to make up for its shameful efforts to stop humanitarian intervention into

Rwanda during the genocide by sending a hefty shipment of arms and military training to Paul Kagame's government after the genocide. The US sent $75 million in emergency military assistance to Rwanda in 1994, *after* Kagame drove the government that had perpetrated the Rwandan genocide from power; but when it could have supported efforts to stop the killing, the Clinton administration was instead actively lobbying to withdraw UN forces from the country.[180]

Rwanda would use that military assistance, and continued military training from the US, to invade the DRC, along with Uganda, from the East in 1996. With the US's full backing, Rwanda and Uganda helped Laurent Kabila overthrow the US's former client—the brutal dictator Mobutu Sese Seko who had become less compliant in his old age. Laurent Kabila, who quickly made sweetheart deals with US mining interests, took power in 1997 in what was known as Zaire at that time and renamed it the DRC. And, when Laurent Kabila himself became less compliant, particularly in regard to granting mining contracts to foreign firms, Clinton supported Rwanda and Uganda in moving against him in 1998, and he was successfully removed at the very end of the Clinton administration in January of 1991.[181]

Meanwhile, other African nations invaded the DRC from the West in 1998 to assist Laurent Kabila in resisting the assault from Rwanda and Uganda. This became known as "Africa's First World War," though it received little press here at the time.

Incredibly, the US, under Bill Clinton, would give military training and hardware to *every country* involved in that conflict—including to the DRC itself—even as the conflict escalated and the death toll surged. Thus, in addition to the $75 million given to Rwanda after the genocide, the US gave significant military support to Angola, Burundi, Chad, DRC, Namibia, Rwanda, Sudan, Uganda, and Zimbabwe, all of which had a role in this war against the DRC.[182] And, the Clinton administration continued to give military support and training to Rwanda, Uganda, Namibia, and Zimbabwe even as they continued to occupy, ravage, and plunder the DRC into Clinton's last year in office (2000).[183]

As The World Policy Institute put it succinctly, "[u]nder Clinton's watch approximately three million people in Rwanda and the eastern region of the DRC died, even as US corporations were participating in questionable mining deals in the region." And indeed, it appears that it was US mining interests, rather than any humanitarian concerns, which may have been the motivating factor for Clinton to support the invasion of the DRC, which is known for some of the purest, untapped minerals on earth, including high-grade copper, cobalt, gold, and coltan (which is critical for electronics and cell phones).[184]

One very telling piece of evidence of this is that, "in a classic case of cronyism," as The World Policy Institute puts it, the very first mining company to receive a mining contract from Laurent Kabila right after he seized power was American Mineral Fields (AMF).[185] The notable thing about AMF, as *Forbes* magazine also noted in an article entitled, "Friends In High Places," was that AMF was headquartered in Hope, Arkansas, the hometown of Bill Clinton and had "interesting Clinton Administration connections."[186] For its part, the UN Security Council, in a 2002 report largely ignored by the media, also concluded that the Rwandan and Ugandan occupation of the DRC was not done for humanitarian purposes, but rather to secure mineral wealth there.[187]

Thus, Kagame's troops, with the full knowledge of Bill Clinton and with a massive arms shipment sent by Clinton for the purpose, invaded the DRC, and began murdering civilians by the hundreds, including women and children, and engaging in rape on a mass scale.[188] The troops not only went after Hutus who had fled to refugee camps in the DRC, but also

Congolese as well. And, Kagame, along with the US-backed Ugandan military as well, has continued his rampage through the DRC with the knowledge, acquiescence, and support of the United States.

All told, nearly six million people have been murdered in the DRC since 1996,[189] and Bill Clinton bears a large responsibility helping to set this slaughter in motion, with, of course, George W. Bush and Barack Obama continuing what Clinton had started and with the plunder of the DRC's resources continuing to this day. And Clinton did so though all the while trumpeting his human rights bona fides. In the end, though, as one commentator on the *Huffington Post* summarized,[190] "According to Human Rights Watch, Clinton's foreign policy generally adopted a 'selective approach to human rights,' turning a 'blind eye in African countries considered to be strategically or economically important.'" Indeed!

As a consequence of the Congo War, Rwanda and Uganda's economies boomed from coltan and cobalt, and Western corporations such as American Mineral Fields and Barrick Gold (whose board included George H.W. Bush and former Canadian Prime Minister Brian Mulroney), received concessions for mining and mineral resources worth over $157 billion.

As Kambale Musavuli, a Congolese activist with Friends of the Congo, also explains, it has been US economic and geopolitical interests which have motivated its continuing support for the bloodbath in the Congo:

> Economic interests in Congo are that which we need in our daily life. The coltan which comes out the Congo can be found in your cell phone, the cobalt of the Congo can be found in the battery of the broker of Congo's minerals, and they loot Congo's mineral resources while they commit atrocities. . . . Chaos allows resources to leave from the Congo at a cheap

price, and of course it's not actually just leaving, it's actually being stolen from the Congolese people.

The second [factor] is military interest. The militaries of Rwanda and Uganda have both been trained by the United States. Since the era when the American soldier was killed in Somalia in Mogadishu, the US did not want to have any of the troops in Africa anymore. So the US created a system in which they would train all the foreign military missions. I mean, can you imagine that . . . today, we have Ugandan soldiers in Afghanistan fighting the war on terror. How many Americans know that? We have Rwandan soldiers in Haiti and in Sudan. These missions can be deployed across the world to protect US interests around the world. . . .

Kambale, speaking for himself and many other Congolese, decries the silence which has allowed the nightmare in the DRC to unfold:

If you are aware, just as we took action to end the Holocaust in Europe, if we know in the Congo millions have died from—estimates take the number to over 6 million, and half of them are children under the age of 5—and we remain silent when we know what is happening, we are really complicit. And in a very tangible way because we are supporting the two oppressive regimes in Rwanda and Uganda, and in turn these nations are using the support that we are giving them to create, fabricate militia groups which are committing war crimes and crimes against humanity.

6

BRAZIL

As Noam Chomsky and Edward S. Herman explained in their landmark book, *The Washington Connection and Third World Fascism*,[191] "[b]etween 1960 and 1969, 11 constitutionally elected governments [in Latin America] were displaced with military dictatorships," with varying degrees of assistance from the United States. One of the more tragic examples of such "displacements" was in Brazil in 1964.

Brazil was a particular problem for Washington given the rise of Liberation Theology in that country after the Second Vatican Council in 1962 which democratized the Church and encouraged its reaching out to the masses of poor in the world. Chomsky and Herman explain that, particularly in Brazil, the changes brought about by this new opening led the Church there to turn away from its old allegiances to elite and to the military, and to begin advocating for and ministering to the poor. That is, it began to advocate for "the preferential treatment of the poor"—the main tenet of Liberation Theology.

Even more troubling, the Brazilian Church began to criticize the role of the US itself in Latin America. As Chomsky and Herman explain, "[t]he church has also become more clear-eyed and explicit on the class bias and massive inhumanity of the development model of growth, and on the role of the US and its military and economic interests in bringing into existence and sustaining the subfascist state." Such a position was simply unacceptable to the US and its leaders.

The Church in Brazil found a friend for its emerging philosophy in Joao Goulart, who was elected president in 1961. Goulart himself, allied with the radical labor movement and left-wing parties, wanted an independent Brazil which would do more for the poor and working people and which would not be subject to the dictates of Washington's regressive economic model of development. As one account explains, "[t]he Goulart regime of 1961–1964 represented the 'fundamental contradiction between a government's responsibility to the citizens who elected it, and the obedience to the demands of foreign creditors expressed in the IMF stabilization program'" which required austerity measures that squeezed the people economically to allow for the payment of the country's foreign debt.[192] And, "[a] government which refuses to make any gesture toward meeting their conditions frequently finds its international credit for imports cut off which, in turn, increases the likelihood of a CIA-induced right-wing coup."[193]

Because Goulart had inherited a massive foreign debt from prior administrations, this contradiction was particularly keen, and the danger of US meddling particularly great. One president, Getulio Vargas, had already committed suicide in 1954 under the strain of the unjust world economic system which simply made it impossible for Brazil to break out of its cycle of debt and impoverishment. Thus, in his suicide note, he wrote, "'[t]he foreign companies made profits of up to five hundred percent. They demonstrably deprived the state of more than a hundred million dollars by false evaluations of import goods.'"[194]

In truth, the US had already been meddling in Brazil's affairs for years, making the coup against Goulart a near certainty. Thus, as it had been doing in many other countries after WWII to ensure compliance with the world order—a world order controlled by the US which was the only major power in the world not devastated by the war and thus in control of 50 percent of the world's resources at its end—the US established "powerful, centralized police forces" which could be called into service against recalcitrant governments like Goulart's which decided to go their independent path.[195]

As explained in 1969 by *CounterSpy*—a publication founded by Phil Agee, a CIA agent who quit the agency over his disgust with its use of torture in countries like Uruguay, where Agee had been stationed:

> Since the end of World War II, Washington had used it role as policeman of the so-called Free World to justify expanding its influence in the Brazilian forces. Military planning between the two countries was coordinated by a Joint Brazil United States Military Commission (JBUSMC). In 1949, the Pentagon helped Brazil set up and staff the Escola Superior de Guerra (Advanced War College), a carbon copy of the US National War College.
>
> The Advanced War College is responsible for national security studies, development of military strategy, and ideas on nation building . . . . To this day, the college has graduated over three thousand civilians and military managers indoctrinated in a right-wing military ideology and the belief that only the armed forces can lead Brazil to its proper destiny as the great power of Latin America.

In short, before Goulart was even elected, the US had already created a system in which the military would dominate the civilian government, and ruthlessly at times. Brazil suffers from this system even still.

Meanwhile, "[i]n the fall of 1961, just as Joao Goulart was taking over the presidency, the United States began an expanded influx of CIA agents and AID officials into Brazil" to train Brazilian police forces in counterinsurgency techniques. The US began hatching plans to use these security forces and other groups in Brazil to destabilize and then overthrow Goulart shortly thereafter.

A very good summary of the US's game plan against Goulart, begun under John and Bobby Kennedy, and continued under Johnson, appeared recently in the magazine of the North American Congress on Latin America (NACLA):

> Washington's long-term efforts in Brazil and elsewhere to undermine movements springing from lower class aspirations and strengthen groups favorable to US investors were infused with a sense of urgency when João ("Jango") Goulart assumed the presidency of Brazil in 1961. Declassified documents released recently by the National Security Archive reveal that officials of the Kennedy Administration were perturbed by Goulart's proposed social reforms and contemplated promoting a military coup. . . .
>
> Accelerating under the Johnson Administration, destabilization of the Goulart government involved the concerted effort of US government agencies in collaboration with the multinational corporate community and international financial institutions. While banks withdrew investments and withheld credit, the CIA, the Agency for International Development, and US businesses channeled funds to political candidates, state governors, police and paramilitary groups, labor unions, media companies, and others inclined to plot against the federal government. Supporters of the government faced an elaborate campaign of divide and suppress, co-opt or conquer.
>
> U.S. military attachés encouraged and coordinated factions of the Brazilian military in plotting a coup d'état. And in case Brazilian military conspirators should begin to falter, the United States had a naval carrier task force standing by.[196]

The CIA's efforts in Brazil during this period went beyond the mere funding of political candidates as above-described to actually hijacking vast swaths of the Brazilian government from top to bottom. Thus, "part of the CIA's effort to create anti-Goulart sentiment in Brazil was the rigging of elections. Working through a front group called the Instituto Brasileiro de Acao Democratica (IBAD), the CIA channeled money into local political campaigns. . . . In the 1962 elections, IBAD not only funded more than one thousand candidates but recruited them so that their first allegiance would be with IBAD and the CIA. At every level, from state deputies up to governorships, the CIA stacked the ballots in favor of candidates."[197]

So thoroughly did the CIA control the Brazilian government, even before Goulart was ousted, that a February 1964 Brazilian investigation into the CIA's election rigging (which the CIA spent $20 million on, that is, $160 million in today's dollars) was suppressed by the very committee doing the investigation. The committee did so because five of its nine members were on the CIA payroll.[198]

When Goulard was finally ousted according to plan by the military on March 31, 1964, "[t]he White House recognized the new government in Brazil with indecent haste, on 2 April 1964."[199] The coup brought much joy to Washington, including to Bobby Kennedy who was still angry with Goulard for refusing his demands in 1962 to remove leftists from his government, restructure the economy in the interest of foreign capital, and relent from nationalizing businesses such as an ITT subsidiary. Kennedy responded upon hearing of the news of the coup, "'[w]ell, Goulart got what was coming to him' . . . ."[200]

The people of Brazil, however, were not so happy, as "[t]he subsequent militocracy saw many thousands exiled, purged, imprisoned, tortured, and/or murdered by death squads."[201] A recently declassified US Department of State document dated

June 8, 1971, discusses the proliferation of death squads linked
to the Brazilian police.[202] As the Department of State explained,
press reports of these death squads (in Portuguese, *Esquadrão da
Morte* (EM)), did not start appearing until 1964—that is, the year
of the coup.

The State Department explained that the EM were an open
secret to which the Brazilian authorities turned a blind eye.
According to the State Department, by the writing of this document in 1971, about eight hundred people had been killed by the
EM, and all of the killings had the following characteristics in
common: "the victims are almost always *marginais* [marginals]";
they are shot multiple times and tied with nylon cords; "the bodies are left in deserted places in the early morning"; a sign with
the EM symbol is left with the corpse; calls are made to the press
telling where the body may be found; and "the police don't question any suspects and the case is closed for lack of evidence." As
the State Department explained, "the vast majority of the victims
. . . have been from the poorest classes, those with the least ability
or predilection to protest." In short, the death squads carried out
a war against the poor.

The military dictatorship, which the US helped bring to
power in 1964 and then backed till its bitter end, lasted until
1985, and continues to haunt Brazil to this day. As far as the US
was concerned, it was an unmitigated success as it successfully
protected the interests of the elite and foreign corporations to the
great detriment of the masses. As Chomsky and Herman explain:

> The military regime has encouraged and subsidized the shift
> to export crops such as soybeans and cattle, without the slight-
> est concern, provision, or consideration for the (non-existent)
> opportunities for the millions of dispossessed:
>> Their lands, houses and crops are wiped out by the sav-
>> age growth of latifundia and big agribusiness. Their living

and working conditions are becoming more difficult. In a tragic contradiction, in which the government economic favors multiply herd of cattle and enlarge plantations, the small laborer sees his family's food supply diminishing.

Volkswagon, Rio Tinto Zinc, Swift Meat Packing, and others have been receiving tax write-offs to develop cattle ranches, while the indigenous people are written off in the process by their government.

The military dictatorship also pleased its US backers by violently cracking down on movements for social justice, and in particular on the upstart Liberation Church and its demands to take care of the poor and oppressed. Again, Chomsky and Herman:

Efforts to organize the peasantry, even for limited self-help activities, have been viewed with the deepest suspicion by the leaders of subfascism, and this form of subversion has led to the arrest, harassment and exile of numerous clergy in Brazil and elsewhere in the empire.

Bishop Casadaliga was the first of many Brazilian bishops to be subject to military interrogation. Many have suffered more severely. Dom Adriano Hipolito, the Bishop of Nova Iguazu, who has often denounced the Brazilian Anti-Communist Alliance (AAB) as a 'bunch of thugs directed and protected by the police' was kidnapped by the AAB, beaten, stripped, painted red, and left lying on a deserted road. And, in October, 1976, Father Joao Brunier, who had gone to the police station with Bishop Casadaliga to protest the torture of two peasant women, was simply shot dead by a policeman . . . . Hundreds of priests and higher officials of the Latin American churches have been tortured, murdered or driven into exile [by US-backed client states]. Six aides of Archbishop [Dom Helder] Camara have been murdered, and he is quite aware that only his international reputation has so far saved him from a similar fate.

The US State Department was well aware of such persecution as recently declassified documents show. For example, a memo from the American Consulate dated December 10, 1969, describes seven Dominican seminarians who were arrested on "terrorism" charges because of their advocacy for "social and economic justice."[203] Another memo dated March 6, 1972, describes a meeting between a number of US officials and Dom Benedito Ulboa Viera, the Auxiliary Bishop of Sao Paulo.[204] This memo describes Bishop Ulboa's thoughts about Church-State relations after four years of military dictatorship:

> The Bishop said that, rather than diminishing, political repression and torture were increasing in Brazil. Even the techniques of torture had been refined and had become more scientific. The security forces were controlled by men who believed that the end of maintaining a communist-free Brazil justified any means; they looked upon the church as a defender of communism, hence an enemy of national security. He had recently gained confidential access to a 'lengthy secret report' on the church prepared by the Second Army and initialed on each page [by] the Commanding General, Humberto Souza e Mello. The burden of the report was that the church was aiding and abetting communism.
>
> The 'fascist' attitudes of those in power prevented any kind of acceptable relationship between the regime and the church. . . . The church must look upon the present government as a 'threat' and within the clergy and among the bishops there was great solidarity in facing this threat.

The memo goes on to describe particular instances in which Catholic students were arrested and tortured by the regime.

I had the honor of hearing Brazilian Archbishop Dom Helder Camara speak at the University of Dayton in the late 1980s. Archbishop Camara was one of the intellectual founders of Liberation Theology and famously said, "When I give food to the poor, they call me a saint. When I ask why they are poor, they call me a communist." In this short statement, Camara summed up the problem the US had with the Liberation Church, and why it had to snuff it out—because it asked pesky questions about the unjust economic order which benefits the US to the detriment of everyone else.

Curiously, the US Embassy in Brazil wrote a memo to the US Department of State in Washington in December of 1977 in which it goes into great detail about a speech given by Archbishop Camara at that time to seven hundred law students in Brasilia.[205] The memo notes that Camara was critical of then-President Jimmy Carter for claiming to be interested in human rights when he was turning a blind eye to the massive human rights abuses going on in Brazil at that time. Camara took Carter to task for overlooking human rights in countries in which it had a strategic interest, such as Brazil.

The US was largely successful in ridding the world of this philosophy, with the US Army School of the Americas bragging that it helped to defeat Liberation Theology.[206]

Meanwhile, though the Brazilians had a short respite from right-wing oppression and austerity under two leaders who themselves had been jailed under the military dictatorship—Presidents Luiz Inacio Lula da Silva and Dilma Rousseff of the PT (Workers Party)—the rightists are on the ascent, having impeached Rousseff and jailed the wildly popular Lula on flimsy charges in what many have called a "legal coup."

The US had a hand in the takedown of Lula and Dilma, and for the same reasons the US intervened against Goulart. As the award-winning investigative online journal, *Consortium News*, has explained:

> The significance of this historical record is the demonstration that the last time Brazil had a "mildly social democratic" government [Goulart], the US cooperated in its removal. The next social democratic government would be the now removed PT government of Presidents Luiz Inacio Lula da Silva and Dilma Rousseff.
>
> Since Lula da Silva took office in 2003, government policies have been credited for lifting millions of Brazilians out of poverty and making Brazil a powerful independent player on the world stage.
>
> In 2009, Lula da Silva was a key figure in the creation of the BRICS organization of emerging economies (Brazil, Russia, India, China and South Africa), representing a challenge to the dominance of the U.S.-based International Monetary Fund and the World Bank. Among other initiatives, BRICS has called for a new global reserve currency, a direct threat to the power of the US dollar.[207]

Such blatant support for the poor, coupled with an audacious assertion of independence in the US's own "backyard," is simply unacceptable. And so, the US, through its Department of Justice (DOJ), has worked hand-in-glove with Brazilian prosecutors in an "anti-corruption" crusade known as *Lava Jato* to target progressive leaders such as Lula and Dilma while ushering in the truly corrupt Brazilian politicians, and sympathizers with the military dictatorship, to power.

As an exposé in *Truthdig* explains:

> Despite public ignorance and its root in the media blindspot on this matter, US involvement in Brazil's Anti-Corruption

Operation Lava Jato, which has already resulted in $3bn payout to North American investors, is not some fringe theory, as some like to pretend—US Acting Attorney General Kenneth Blanco has publicly boasted about it himself:

"It is hard to imagine a better cooperative relationship in recent history than that of the United States Department of Justice and the Brazilian prosecutors. We have cooperated and substantially assisted one another on a number of public matters that have now been resolved, and are continuing to do so on a number of ongoing investigations.

The cooperation between the Department and Brazil has led to extraordinary results. . . . Indeed, just this past week, the prosecutors in Brazil won a guilty verdict against former President Lula da Silva . . . ."[208]

As noted in a recent letter to *The Guardian* by a number of noted British professors, "[t]here is overwhelming evidence of his [Lula's] innocence and that he has been tried unfairly and imprisoned so as to deny his legitimate right to stand in October's presidential elections, where he is currently leading in the polls. Legal experts in Brazil and around the world have pointed to the irregularities of his trial and the questionable circumstances of his imprisonment."[209] The United Nations Human Rights Committee has even ruled that Brazil must allow the imprisoned Lula to stand for reelection—an election he would be certain to win—but the current government is refusing to honor this demand.[210]

But this is all quite acceptable to the US which has weaponized anti-corruption prosecutions to remove politicians it does not like from contention. Incredibly, the US DOJ is able to sideline such politicians even in other countries thousands of miles away. The reverse—for example, Russia helping prosecute and impeach politicians in the US—would simply be unthinkable, and quite rightly so.

The joint US–Brazil *Lavo Jato* program also led to the impeachment of President Dilma, whose personal phone conversations were intercepted and taped by the Obama administration,[211] from office. The absurdity of her impeachment for alleged corruption was well-expressed by David Miranda in an opinion piece in London's *The Guardian* newspaper, entitled, "The real reason Dilma Rousseff's enemies want her impeached"

> It is impossible to convincingly march behind a banner of "anti-corruption" and "democracy" when simultaneously working to install the country's most corruption-tainted and widely disliked political figures. . . .
>
> A *New York Times* article last week reported that "60% of the 594 members of Brazil's Congress"—the ones voting to impeach Rousseff—"face serious charges like bribery, electoral fraud, illegal deforestation, kidnapping and homicide". By contrast, said the article, Rousseff "is something of a rarity among Brazil's major political figures: she has not been accused of stealing for herself".
>
> Last Sunday's televised, raucous spectacle in the lower house received global attention because of some repellent (though revealing) remarks made by impeachment advocates. One of them, prominent right-wing congressman Jair Bolsonaro— widely expected to run for president and who a recent poll shows is the leading candidate among Brazil's richest—said he was casting his vote in honour of a human-rights-abusing colonel in Brazil's military dictatorship who was personally responsible for Rousseff's torture [while in jail for organizing against the dictatorship]. His son, Eduardo, proudly cast his vote in honour of "the military men of '64"—the ones who led the coup.[212]

In other words, in typical fashion, the US, in the name of "democracy promotion," is helping bring about a coup very like the one it helped give birth to in 1964, and with the same results—results which, while horrifying for the people of Brazil, are quite advantageous to the US's interest of maximizing its exploitation of Brazil.

Thus, the removal of Dilma from office paved the way for the the privatization of Brazil's national oil company, Petrobras, and its "being sold off for cents to foreign producers such as US Chevron & ExxonMobil, UK's BP & Shell, and Norway's Statoil, at an estimated loss of R$1 trillion—funds once earmarked by Dilma Rousseff for a revolution in public education & health investment," and to the "decimation of workers rights and overhaul of the pension system, all demanded by Wall Street . . . ."[213] And the sidelining of Lula in prison guarantees that these processes will not be reversed.

At the same time, the ousting of Lula and Dilma has allowed for the security forces and paramilitary groups to wipe out land rights and indigenous activists through mass murder. In 2017 alone, fifty-seven land rights activists were murdered throughout Brazil, and such slaughter was the direct consequence of the weakening of institutions which Lula and Dilma created to protect them. Thus, as the *LA Times* recently explained:

> According to Global Witness, a nongovernmental organization that tracks the exploitation of indigenous people and their resources, 2017 was not only the most lethal year on record for environmental activists in Brazil, but one of the deadliest in any country. Global Witness said its tally in Brazil is probably an undercount because its methodology requires that it identify each victim by name, which can be a challenge because some potential victims live in highly isolated areas.
>
> The peril for land defenders in Brazil is not expected to improve anytime soon, the group says.
>
> "On paper, Brazil has many of the policies and institutions that could solve this problem and protect the rights

and well-being of ordinary Brazilians, but this government is weakening those institutions in favor of facilitating big business," said Ben Leather, senior campaigner for Global Witness.

In 2017, state agency FUNAI, which is responsible for protecting indigenous peoples' rights in Brazil, had its budget slashed in half, forcing it to close several regional offices. INCRA, the state agency responsible for redistributing land to small-scale farmers and Afro-descendants who live on lands called *quilombos*, had its budget cut by 30%.[214]

The words of Chomsky and Herman about the aftermath of the 1964 military coup are just as applicable to the current situation post-"legal coup": "[t]he state functions to prevent by force any defense of the rural majority and to allow the powerful to violate the already feeble law with impunity."

Meanwhile, the Brazilian military is encroaching more and more into politics and into policing, and is openly threatening another coup. As the *New York Times* wrote in July 2018:[215]

Members of Brazil's armed forces, who have largely stayed out of political life since the end of the military dictatorship 30 years ago, are making their biggest incursion into politics in decades, with some even warning of a military intervention.

Retired generals and other former officers with strong ties to the military leadership are mounting a sweeping election campaign, backing about 90 military veterans running for an array of posts—including the presidency—in national elections this October. . . .

And if the ballot box does not bring change quickly enough, some prominent former generals warn that military leaders may feel compelled to step in and reboot the political system by force.

And so, all is going according to plan for the powers-that-be in the US who have found ways to reproduce the coup d'etat of 1964 in creative ways, destroying democracy and social justice in Brazil once again in the interest of profit.

But of course, the undermining of democracy abroad naturally leads to the urge to undermine democracy at home. Thus, as Chomsky and Herman point out, such politicians as Richard Nixon learned from US meddling in countries like Brazil to do his own meddling in our elections: "[t]he CIA would forge documents to discredit foreign politicians in Brazil and Chile, and the Nixon administration would forge documents to discredit Kennedy or some other enemy politicians. In Brazil, a CIA front organization would use extorted and laundered US money to subsidize amenable politicians, and a scholar on Brazil finds it an 'overwhelming temptation to compare the modus operandi of this organization (a Brazilian front of the CIA), to that of Richard Nixon's Committee for the re-election of the President (CREEP).' Brazil was, in fact, a model for Nixon."

Finally, as I write this chapter, I learn of another land right activist and indigenous leader, Jorginho Guajajara, a leader of the Guajajara people, murdered in Brazil in retaliation for his anti-logging activism.[216] The Amazon he was fighting to protect is literally the lungs of this world, which we depend upon to breathe and survive. His death, which can be attributed to the meddling of our own government in his country's domestic affairs, and other deaths like his, may guarantee that humanity's days on this earth are numbered.

7

VIETNAM

No ACCOUNT OF US ELECTION MEDDLING is complete without a discussion of the US War on Vietnam. This devastating war began with the US's scuttling of elections in Vietnam which could have unified and brought peace to that nation, and it was prolonged for seven years longer than it should have by the treasonous acts of Richard Nixon and his associates who secretly undermined a peace agreement brokered by President Johnson in 1968 in order to win the elections that year. It was Nixon's attempt to cover up this meddling which would ultimately lead to his downfall and the biggest Constitutional crisis in US history.

Before getting to the conduct of the war in Vietnam, it is important to consider the actual reasons the US was there as contrasted with the stated goals. Thus, the US did not send tens of thousands of US soldiers to kill and die in Vietnam in order to defend democracy and freedom, as we are meant to believe. Rather, after World War II (in which the US had received significant help from Ho Chi Minh and his Viet Minh guerilla fighters to fight off Japan) the US initially entered the fray in Vietnam in order to defend French colonialism there.

And, as has been quite typical of the US's willing collaboration with fascists and even Nazis after WWII, the US allied with recently defeated Japan in helping to defeat the Vietnamese independence effort against the French. As John Marciano explains, "[i]n a stunning shift in history, US vessels brought French troops [many of themselves who had just fought on the side of Vichy France] so they could join recently released Japanese troops to support France's attempt to crush the Vietnamese independence movement." Marciano notes that this aroused the very first anti-war protests against the American intervention in Vietnam—this time by US sailors who could not stomach the hypocrisy of what the US was doing and who they were doing it with.

Ultimately, of course, the Viet Minh triumphed against the French in the battle of Dien Bien Phu on May 7, 1954. As Marciano relates, the Viet Minh "had organized and inspired a poor, untrained, ill-equipped population to fight and ultimately win against a far better equipped and trained army" to win their independence. One might believe (and Ho Chi Minh in fact did at one point) that the US, in the Spirit of '76, would welcome and support such an independence victory. Ho Chi Minh even cited the American Declaration of Independence in declaring the independence of Vietnam from France.

Indeed, according to the *New York Times*, in a 1971 article based on the infamous Pentagon Papers, "in late 1945 and early 1946, Ho Chi Minh wrote at least eight letters to President Truman and the State Department requesting American help in winning Vietnam's independence from France." In one of these letters, Ho Chi Minh wrote:

> I assure you of the admiration and friendship we feel toward American people and its representatives here. That such friendly feelings have been exhibited not only to Americans themselves but also to impostors in American uniform is proof that the US stand for international justice and peace is appreciated by the entire Vietnamese nation and "governing spheres".

I convey to you Mr. President and to the American people the expression of our great respect and admiration.[217]

Sadly, none of these letters were responded to. Instead, silence was the rude reply.

Meanwhile, after the Viet Minh victory at Dien Bien Phu, the French and the Viet Minh signed what came to be known as the Geneva Accords—an agreement intended to end the conflict and to guarantee Vietnam's independence. As the *New York Times* explains, an important part of this 1954 agreement provided that Vietnam would be temporarily divided between north and south pending elections to be held in 1956 which would unite Vietnam under one elected leadership.[218] The accord further provided that "[t]he introduction of foreign troops or bases and the use of Vietnamese territory for military purposes were forbidden. The United States, which did not join with the nations that endorsed the accords, issued a declaration taking note of the provisions and promising not to disturb them."[219] But no sooner was this promise made than the US began to actively, and violently, act to unravel the accords and to replace the French as the colonial occupier of Vietnam.

Again, the *New York Times*:

The secret Pentagon study of the Vietnam war discloses that a few days after the Geneva accords of 1954, the Eisenhower Administration's National Security Council decided that the accords were a "disaster" and the President approved actions to prevent further Communist expansion in Vietnam.

These White House decisions, the Pentagon account concludes, meant that the United States had "a direct role in the ultimate breakdown Of the Geneva settlement." . . .

According to the Pentagon writer, the National Security Council, at a meeting on Aug. 8, 1954, just after the Geneva conference, ordered an urgent program of economic and military aid—substituting American advisers for French advisers—to the new South Vietnamese Government of Ngo Dinh Diem.[220]

The accords were seen as a "disaster" by the Eisenhower administration, moreover, because it was quite aware that US ally Diem was horribly unpopular, and that Ho Chi Minh was almost universally beloved. US intelligence revealed that if free elections were held, Ho Chi Minh would be elected the president of a unified Vietnam with about 80 percent of the vote. Democratic elections in Vietnam, therefore, had to be stopped at all costs.

Consequently, as the *Times* explains, "the Eisenhower Administration sent a team of agents to carry out clandestine warfare against North Vietnam from the minute the Geneva conference closed," and to lay the groundwork for future operation. Thus, "the team 'spent the last days of Hanoi in contaminating the oil supply of the bus company for a gradual wreckage of engines in the buses, in taking actions for delayed sabotage of the railroad (which required teamwork with a CIA special technical team in Japan who performed their part brilliantly), and in writing detailed notes of potential targets for future paramilitary operations.'"

And, while the *Times* also explains that the US also began massive economic and military support for the hated Diem regime, it neglected to mention what few are willing to: that the US began to work with Diem in violently assaulting the civilian population, not of North Vietnam, but of its ostensible ally, South Vietnam.

Noam Chomsky has made this point over and over: that especially in the early part of the war on Vietnam, it was South Vietnam which was the target, and not North Vietnam. As he and Edward S. Herman have written, "[u]nder our tutelage, Diem began his own 'search-and-destroy' operations in the mid- and late 1950s, and his prison camps and the torture chambers were filled and active. In 1956 the official figure for political prisoners in South Vietnam was fifteen to twenty thousand."

In addition, Diem engaged in a "pacification program" in South Vietnam. In one "pacification" campaign, according to one-time Diem supporter and adviser Joseph Buttinger, "[h]undreds, perhaps thousands of peasants were killed. Whole villages whose populations were not friendly to the government were destroyed by artillery. These facts were kept secret from the American people." And, this took place at a time, it should be noted, that the Viet Minh in the North were concentrated on political work and were quite restrained in military operations.

As Chomsky and Herman point out:

> Diem's extensive use of violence and reprisals against for-
> mer Resistance fighters was in direct violation of the Geneva
> Accords (Article 14c), as was his refusal to abide by the election
> proviso. The main reason for Diem's refusal to abide by this
> mode of settlement in 1955–56 was quite evident: the expatriate
> mandarin imported from the United States had minimal pop-
> ular support and little hope for winning in a free election. . . .
> Diem was a typical subfascist tyrant, compensating for lack of
> indigenous support with extra doses of terror. Violence is the
> natural mode of domination for those without local roots or
> any positive strategy for gaining support, in this instance the
> United States and its client regime.

The US and its henchman Diem thereby managed to scut-tle the 1954 Geneva Accords and to prevent the election in 1956 which could have brought peace, democracy, and independence to Vietnam. Instead, Vietnam would be subjected to an unforgiv-ing war fought on a scale never seen before or since.

The gruesomeness of the US war effort in Vietnam is best typified by the My Lai Massacre, which Obama has recently tried to whitewash as the "My Lai Incident." In case the reader never heard of this incident, or possibly forgot about it, here is a little summary of that event which is described in detail in Nick Turse's recent, *Kill Anything That Moves: The Real American War in Vietnam*.[221]

On the evening of March 15, 1968, US soldiers from Company C, or, "Charlie Company" entered the village of My Lai where they were ordered to "kill everything in the village"; "to kill everything that breathed." This admonition included women and children. Indeed, Charlie Company met no armed adversaries that day—just women, children, and the elderly. And so, the Americans "gunned down old men sitting in their homes and children as they ran for cover. Tossed grenades into homes. Shot women and babies at close range." For good measure, "they raped women and young girls, mutilated the dead, systematically burned homes, and fouled the area's drinking water." General Westmoreland congratulated these brave soldiers for their "heavy blows" against the enemy, and their "aggressiveness." All told, over five hundred civilians were killed in this massacre.

As Turse explains, there were many My Lais during the war. Indeed, he cites a letter from a Vietnam veteran named Charles McDuff in which he expressed his disgust over the war in Southeast Asia, saying that My Lai was merely the tip of the iceberg.[222] Indeed, My Lai–type incidents were encouraged by the US military's designation of "free fire zones" in which "everyone, men, women, children, could be considered [a fair target]; you could not be held responsible for firing on innocent civilians since by definition there were none there."[223]

In addition to such atrocities, the US subjected Vietnam to the equivalent of 640 Hiroshima-sized atomic bombs—*the lion's share on South Vietnam which was the US's ally*. Thus, Chomsky and

Herman quote a 1967 letter from a US Marine to Senator William Fulbright, in which he stated:

> 'I went to Vietnam, a hard charging Marine 2nd Lieutenant, sure that I had answered the plea of a victimized people in their struggle against communist aggression. The at believe lasted about two weeks. Instead of fighting communist aggressors I found that 90% of the time our military actions were directed against the people of South Vietnam. These people had little sympathy or for that matter knowledge of the Saigon Government. We engaged in a war in South Vietnam to pound a people into submission to a government that has little or no popular support among the real people of South Vietnam.'[224]

The US even bombed Catholic Churches throughout South Vietnam for good measure.

All told, according to Nick Turse, the US, with its superior air and firepower, killed approximated 3.8 million Vietnamese (8 percent of its total population), and created over fourteen million refugees. Meanwhile, Vietnam continues to feel the effects, in terms of environmental degradation and horrible birth defects, from the "millions of gallons of chemical defoliants, millions of pounds of chemical gases, [and] endless canisters of napalm" which the US dumped on that country.

All of this bloodshed began in Vietnam with the US's interference to prevent democratic elections in 1956. And it would continue when Richard Nixon and Henry Kissinger interfered in 1968 to prevent a peace deal for Vietnam in the interest of ensuring an electoral victory for Nixon in the upcoming US presidential elections.

The 1968 presidential elections, which saw a sitting president, Lyndon Johnson, pressured by anti-war sentiment into bowing out of his reelection bid; the murder of one of its candidates, Bobby

Kennedy, shortly after the assassination of Martin Luther King; the police riot at the Chicago Democratic National Convention; and the Democratic Party's undemocratic anointing of pro-war candidate Hubert Humphrey as their nominee despite the fact that he had not even run in the primaries; was quite possibly the most fraught and significant election in US history since the US Civil War.

While Johnson had decided to abandon his campaign in lieu of suffering an almost certain defeat to anti-war candidate Eugene McCarthy, he nonetheless worked desperately to try to negotiate an end to the Vietnam War—a war which destroyed his presidency, had created mass social unrest, and which was threatening to sink the Democratic Party. Had he succeeded in this goal, Humphrey surely would have defeated Richard Nixon in the election, and US history (*sans* Watergate for example) might look very different today. Nixon understood this, and so he hatched a plan to secretly scuttle Johnson's efforts.

As John A. Farrell recently wrote in an article entitled, "When a Candidate Conspired With a Foreign Power to Win an Election,"[225] in October of 1968, Nixon and his campaign chief of staff, H.R. Haldeman, moved forward on a plot to "sabotage Johnson's plans to stage productive peace talks, so that a frustrated American electorate would turn to the Republicans as their only hope to end the war." And, a key person to assist in this plan was none other than Henry Kissinger who was actually serving as Johnson's foreign policy adviser, and who would serve as a spy for Nixon at this time. Kissinger, who worked with Nixon to kill peace in Vietnam, would be handsomely rewarded later by Nixon with a post as national security adviser and then secretary of State.

Another key asset was Anna Chennault, a Republican fundraiser with strong ties to then–South Vietnamese President Nguyen Van Thieu. Thieu had succeeded Diem as president after the CIA had Diem killed in November of 1963. In what became known as the "Chennault Affair," Nixon reached out to Thieu through Chennault to "'monkey wrench'" Johnson's negotiations by prevailing upon Thieu to hold firm in prosecuting the war and in abandoning the peace talks by promising him a better deal if he were elected.

As Farrell writes, "[t]he Nixon campaign's sabotage of Johnson's peace process was successful. . . . Thieu's decision to boycott the talks headlined the *New York Times* and other US newspapers, reminding American voters of their long-harbored mistrust of the wheeler-dealer LBJ and his 'credibility gap' on Vietnam."

Nixon went on to win the 1968 elections, but at a terrible price. As an initial matter, Nixon most assuredly violated US law, namely the Logan Act which forbids US citizens from corresponding with "'any foreign government . . . in relation to any disputes or controversies with the United States, or to defeat the measures of the United States . . . .'"[226]

More significantly, by the time of the 1968 election, over thirty thousand US servicemen had already been killed in Vietnam. Another twenty thousand would die thereafter during the Nixon administration.[227]

Meanwhile, the Vietnamese would suffer another seven years of brutal war, and some of its worst years. For example, it was just after the failure of the peace talks and the election of Richard Nixon that General Julian Ewell, the US 9th Division commander who would become known as "the butcher of the Delta," initiated what he termed "Speedy Express."[228] Speedy Express, which would run from December 1968 to May of 1969, was an operation intended to subdue the Mekong Delta region of South Vietnam, and it became a massive bloodbath by design.

As Nick Turse explains, in carrying out this operation, "the United States brought to bear every option in its arsenal" to

attack the Delta, increasing the kill rate, mostly of civilians, dra-
matically, from twenty-four Vietnamese to one US serviceman at
the beginning of the operation to 134 to one by the end. Many
of the kills were had through aerial attacks at night which did
not distinguish between combatants or noncombatants, men
or women, adults or children. As senior adviser Louis Janowski
would explain, the operation, which involved almost 6,500 air
strikes "dropping at least 5,078 tons of bombs and 1,784 tons of
napalm," amounted to a form of "'nonselective terrorism.'"

S. Brian Willson, then an Air Force captain and now a peace
activist living in Nicaragua, told an interviewer:

> 'It was the height of immorality . . . . One of the times I counted
> bodies after an air strike—which always ended with two napalm
> bombs which would just fry everything that was left—I counted
> sixty-two bodies. In my report I described them as so many
> women between fifteen and twenty-five and so many children—
> usually in their mothers' arms or very close to them—and so
> many old people.' When he later read the official tally of dead,
> he found that it listed them as 130 VC [Viet Cong combatants]
> killed.[229]

Nixon's treachery, which illegally hijacked US democracy,
also prevented the Vietnamese from being spared such a terrible fate. It also prevented them from being spared of suffering
under the cruelty of another US operation, the CIA's "Phoenix
Program," which was run with its greatest ferocity between 1968
and 1972 and which valued "body counts" over all else. Under
this program, over twenty thousand Vietnamese, very few of any
strategic significance and most of them completely innocent,
were captured, tortured, and assassinated.[230]

In addition, the North Vietnamese were subjected to the
devastating 1973 "Christmas bombing" which Thieu apparently

prevailed upon Nixon to order by using the leverage he had gained in 1968 by helping Nixon win the election.[231]

All told, possibly an additional one million Vietnamese were killed after the 1968 breakdown of peace talks caused by Nixon's machinations.[232]

Moreover, during Nixon's presidency, the war against Vietnam was expanded, for some time without the knowledge of the American people, to neighboring countries who also suffered immensely. Thus, Nixon expanded the war to neighboring Laos, reducing about one quarter of the population of three million to refugees, and subjecting another one-third of the population to the most intense bombardment in history.

The war was also expanded to the then very peaceful country of Cambodia in 1969, very shortly after Nixon came to office. The US subjected Cambodia as well to merciless bombing. As one source described the scene, "'[t]he methodical sacking of economic resources, of rubber plantations and factories, of rice fields and forests, of peaceful and delightful villages which disappeared one after another beneath the bombs and napalm, has no military justification and serves essentially to starve the population.'"[233]

In addition, the CIA sponsored a right-wing coup in Cambodia in 1970 which brought Lon Nol to power. As Chomsky and Herman have related, "Lon Nol quickly organized a pogrom-bloodbath against local Vietnamese" who had fled the war in their home country.[234] Over five thousand people were killed in this slaughter, with three hundred thirty thousand more Vietnamese forced out of the country. The US and South Vietnam would then invade "to support the organizers of the slaughter, who were on the verge of being overthrown."

Of course, as we know, this massive slaughter in Cambodia radicalized some of the population, including the infamous Pol Pot, and led directly to the "killing fields" of the Khmer Rouge. And lest we forget, while the US initially opposed the Khmer

Rouge, it was not the US which ousted them from power, but the Vietnamese. As commentator Gregory Elich opined, the Vietnamese 1978 campaign against the Khmer Rouge "was one of history's great liberations."[235] Historian Eric Hobsbawm agrees, pointing to the general "consensus" that this was an "obvious" case of "justified intervention."[236] And so, of course, the US had to oppose it, and to support the one force that could continue to harass the Vietnamese and the new government in Cambodia—the Khmer Rouge—and the US did so for many years to come.[237]

Meanwhile, it was Nixon's desperate attempt to hide the truth about the nature of the war on Vietnam, as well as the truth about his treasonous acts which got him into the White House to begin with, which would lead to the Watergate scandal and the greatest Constitutional crisis in US history. Indeed, the team of "plumbers" Nixon ordered to break in to the Watergate building were initially assembled to break in to the Brookings Institute in order to retrieve a file that Johnson had kept on his interference in the peace talks.[238] The "plumbers," under the direction of E. Howard Hunt, would also break into the psychiatric offices of Daniel Ellsberg—the whistleblower who leaked the Pentagon Papers which revealed the cruel nature and futility of the Vietnam War—in order to try to discredit Ellsberg.

How poetic then, as John A. Farrell wrote in his piece on the "Chennault Affair," that Anna Chennault would live on for many years at the Watergate building to and through Nixon's resignation from office and the end of the Vietnam War.

In other words, one act of meddling led to another, many times to cover up or mitigate the damage done by the first act of meddling. If there is any true domino theory, it is this one, and it is one which the US has yet to come to terms with. Democracy in multiple countries, including our own, was greatly undermined by the initial meddling in Vietnam to preserve imperial domination. And the cause of democracy would be undermined time and time again in this pursuit to dominate other peoples.

Meanwhile, what became of Nixon's promise to Thieu that he could get him a better deal if he held out for a Nixon presidency to negotiate a peace deal? This too came to naught. As Robert Parry explains, "in the end, Nixon accepted a peace deal in late 1972 similar to what Johnson was negotiating in 1968. And the final outcome was not changed. After US troops departed, the South Vietnamese government soon fell to the North and the Vietcong." And yet, the lives of millions were destroyed in the meantime, and for absolutely nothing.

The Democratic Party, in its National Platform of 1900, spoke this profound truth when it stated: "We assert that no nation can long endure half republic and half empire, and we warn the American people that imperialism abroad will quickly lead and inevitably, to despotism at home."[239] It is sad that we have yet to heed these words.

8

CHILE

ON SEPT. 11, 1973, GENERAL AUGUSTO Pinochet led a violent coup against the elected government of President (and medical doctor) Salvador Allende, bringing an end to democratic rule in that country for the next sixteen-plus years. Many refer to this as the "First 9/11," and it would be much more devastating than the 9/11 the US suffered in 2001 in terms of its body count and historical significance for a number of countries.

At the time of the coup, Chile had been the longest-standing constitutional democracy in Latin America—something the United States would generally claim to support. However, because the United States did not like the left-leaning (but not Communist) Dr. Allende, it chose to help foment the coup that toppled his government and then continue to support the Pinochet dictatorship even as its human rights crimes became apparent. General Pinochet's regime ultimately was responsible for the murder of at least 3,197 individuals and the torture of over thirty thousand.[240]

The CIA had been intervening in Chile for years, and was indeed successful in blocking an earlier election bid by Salvador Allende back in 1964. As Peter Kornbluh, in his book *The Pinochet File*, based on declassified CIA documents, explains, the US spent billions of dollars, starting in 1961, to try to prevent

Salvador Allende and his Popular Unity coalition from being elected.

This included $2.6 million in funds to directly bankroll the 1964 election campaign of Eduardo Frei and his Christian Democratic Party, and $3 million in anti-Allende black ops during this same campaign. Quoting the Senator Frank Church Committee which investigated CIA wrongdoing in the early '70s, the CIA's black ops included the following:

> "Extensive use was made of the press, radio, films, pamphlets, posters, leaflets, direct mailing, paper streamers and wall paintings. It was a 'scare campaign' that relied heavily on images of Soviet tanks and Cuban firing squads and was directed especially to women. Hundreds of thousands of copies of the anti-communist pastoral letter of Pope Pius XI were distributed by Christian Democratic organizations. . . . 'Disinformation' and 'black propaganda'—material which purported to originate from another source, such as the Chilean Communist Party—were used as well."[241]

And when these CIA efforts propelled Eduardo Frei to the presidency, the US really turned on the spigot. Thus, to make sure Frei stayed in power, the US provided "over 1.2 billion in economic grants and loans—an astronomical amount for that era."[242] That is almost $9 billion in today's dollars. In addition, "[a]lthough Chile faced no internal or external security threat," the US provided $91 in military assistance to Chile between 1962 and 1970. As Kornbluh notes, this military assistance had one goal in mind—"to establish closer ties to the Chilean generals" in case later elections produced undesired results. And indeed, that insurance plan would soon be needed.

Thus, despite the expenditure of another $2 million in covert funds to influence the 1970 elections, Salvador Allende came out on top. In response, the CIA then moved to try to prevent Allende from ever taking office. Thus, a September 19, 2000, document released by the CIA revealed that the CIA "sought to instigate a [military] coup" against Mr. Allende even before he took office in 1970.[243] And the decision to prevent the inauguration of Allende came from the president of the United States himself, Richard Nixon.

The notes of Nixon's directive, taken by the director of the CIA, Richard Helms, state:[244]

- 1 in 10 chance perhaps, but save Chile!
- worth spending
- not concerned risks involved
- no involvement of embassy
- $10,000,000 available, more if necessary
- full-time job—best men we have
- game plan
- make economy scream
- 48 house for plan of action

As declassified documents show, "[t]he CIA pursued a basic three-step plan: (1) identify, contact, and collect intelligence on coup-minded officers; (2) inform them that the US was committed to 'full support in coup' short of sending the marines; (3) foster the creation of 'a coup climate by propaganda, disinformation, and terrorist activities' to provide a stimulus and pretext for the military to move.'"[245]

However, all of these steps combined were to add up to one thing: chaos. As a chilling Top Secret CIA cable from Santiago, Chile, on October 10, 1970, sums it all up: "*Carnage could be considerable and prolonged, i.e., civil war. . . . You have asked us to provoke chaos in Chile . . . we provide you with formula for chaos which is unlikely to be bloodless.*'" (emphasis in text).[246] This goal of creating chaos in an otherwise peaceful, democratic, and hitherto allied nation can only be viewed as evil; as the very worst fate one country could attempt to visit upon another. But this was not only the goal of the US in Chile; it was and remains the goal of the US in many other targeted countries, as this book attempts to detail.

Meanwhile, as the CIA relates, it "was working with three different groups of plotters," all of which "made it clear that any coup would require the kidnapping of army Cmdr. Rene Schneider, who felt deeply that the constitution required that the army allow Allende to assume power."[247]

The CIA, not having any qualms about constitutionality or civilian rule, admits that it agreed with the assessment that the kidnapping (though it claims not killing) of Schneider was necessary, and so it provided weapons and $50,000 in cash for the kidnapping operation.[248] The plan was to raise a "false flag" by then blaming the kidnapping on the Communists. Not surprisingly, the kidnapping operation ended in the killing of Schneider when he tried to defend himself. The path was now being paved for the military overthrow of Allende.

The CIA continued to assist the coup-plotters through the time Dr. Allende was overthrown. The overthrow of Allende was particularly brutal, and laden with symbolism, with air force planes bombing the Presidential Palace and killing Allende in the process. The message was clear—democracy itself was under attack on that day.

The *Washington Post* would later explain the series of events in which the CIA was a key player:

> In Chile, the United States prevented Allende from winning an election in 1964. "A total of nearly four million dollars was spent on some fifteen covert action projects, ranging from organizing slum dwellers to passing funds to political parties," detailed a Senate inquiry in the mid-1970s that started

to expose the role of the CIA in overseas elections. When it couldn't defeat Allende at the ballot box in 1970, Washington decided to remove him anyway.

"I don't see why we need to stand by and watch a country go communist due to the irresponsibility of its own people," Kissinger is said to have quipped. Pinochet's regime presided over years of torture, disappearances and targeted assassinations.[249]

As another *Washington Post* story summarized, in September of 1973, "the Chilean military, aided by training and financing from the US Central Intelligence Agency, gained absolute control of the country in less than a week. The new regime waged raids, executions, 'disappearances' and the arrest and torture of thousands of Chilean citizens - establishing a climate of fear and intimidation that would remain for years to come."[250]

In addition to the CIA, another key actor in the coup was the International Telephone and Telegraph Company (ITT), which wanted Allende gone for fear that he might be a threat to their interests in Chile. ITT, which was also involved in the military coup in Brazil in 1964 and which owned 70 percent of the Chilean Telephone Company as well as The Sheraton Hotel at the time, backed Allende's opponents in the 1970 elections and provided crucial financial support to the coup plotters against Allende.[251]

Shortly before the coup in which he would die, Dr. Allende gave an impassioned speech at the UN decrying the interference of ITT, as well as Kennecott Copper, in his country:

Two firms that are part of the central nucleus of the large transnational companies that sunk their claws into my country, the International Telegraph and Telephone Company and the Kennecott Copper Corporation, tried to run our political life.

ITT, a huge corporation whose capital is greater than the budget of several Latin American nations put together and greater than that of some industrialized countries, began, from the very moment that the people's movement was victorious in the elections of September 1970, a sinister action to keep me from taking office as President.

With the urging of the CIA, the plan that ITT put into place, along with corporations like Anaconda and Kennecott copper companies, was to strangle the Chilean economy—in the words of Nixon himself, to "make [the] economy scream." As left-wing economist Zoltan Zigedy recently wrote upon the forty-fifth anniversary of the 1973 coup against Allende:

> Credits and loans were denied. The global price of copper (70–80% of Chilean exports) was manipulated downward to deny Chile's government essential revenue for the country's social programs (salaries rose between 35% and 66% in 1971) and industrial development.
>
> Without hard currency, outside loans or revenue from trade, hyperinflation eventually plagued Chile, reaching 163% in 1973.
>
> "The US credit and trade squeeze was designed for a political purpose . . . : to promote the political demise of a democratic socialist government. Economic pressures led to economic dislocations (scarcities), which generated the social basis (discontent among the middle class) that created the political context for a military coup."
>
> Funding middle class truck-owners' "strikes" through the CIA and AIFLD [the AFL-CIO's international wing] further fueled middle class alienation . . . .[252]

Of course, this strategy of making the economy of a country targeted for regime "scream," and then blaming the targeted government for the resulting woes of the people, is a tried-and-true one of the US.

For example, as discussed earlier, the US ran this game plan in Iran to great effect to topple the government of Prime Minister Mosaddegh, and it is doing this right now to try to topple the current government of Iran. Thus, with the connivance of its good friend Saudi Arabia—not exactly the paragon of democracy and human rights in the world—the US has helped to artificially depress the price of oil with the express intention of undermining the economy of Iran.[253]

In addition, the US has imposed economic sanctions intended to destroy the Iranian economy, cause suffering to all sectors of society, and thereby cause unrest and anti-government foment. As the *LA Times* explains:

> Economic analysts say the sanctions will spread misery across Iran's economy—worsening inflation, accelerating the decline of the currency, making imports scarcer and making medicine, in particular, more difficult to acquire. . . .
>
> As with the previous sanctions regime, these penalties are likely to hit working-class and low-income families the hardest, said Esfandyar Batmanghelidj, founder of Bourse & Bazaar, a publication that tracks Iran's economy. . . .
>
> Wealthier families will also struggle but are better able to weather the storm, drawing on savings and sourcing some scarce goods—such as medication—from overseas, Batmanghelidj said.[254]

The US is doing the very same to Venezuela. Indeed, the US has been economically attacking Venezuela for nearly twenty years now in order to overturn the government of Hugo Chavez and his successor Nicolas Maduro. In addition to the attack on oil price which itself has devastated the Venezuelan economy,[255] the US has also levied sanctions against Venezuela's oil industry, including freezing billions of dollars of oil revenues from Citgo in the US; supported a management-led oil strike; outlawed US financial institutions from helping Venezuela refinance its debt; and forbade Americans from buying Venezuela's Petro cyber-currency.[256] Combined, this has caused untold suffering for the people of Venezuela, and largely undermined the substantial and unprecedented gains that the Chavista government had made in alleviating poverty.[257] According to economist Mark Weisbrot, these measures "have worsened shortages of medicine and food, in an economy that is already suffering from inflation of about 3,000 percent annually and a depression that has cost about 38 percent of GDP."[258]

All of this, of course, has been aimed at creating regime change. Indeed, the US is open about this. Thus, to try to influence the 2018 Venezuelan presidential elections—elections I observed in Caracas—President Trump, in addition to threatening the main opposition candidate with sanctions if he even ran in the election, threatened that he would impose more sanctions, including possibly cutting off Venezuela oil imports, if Venezuela went to the polls and voted for Nicolas Maduro.[259] Trump also threatened possible military invasion.[260] This is a form of extortion, pure and simple, and there can be no greater way of attempting to influence an election outcome.

In short, the rationales for such quite insidious attacks against other countries may change, and the methods modified somewhat, but what never changes is the US's feeling of entitlement, with generally little resistance by its population or press, to engage in such interventions in order to bring about the government of its choosing.

Meanwhile, back in Chile, the combined efforts of the CIA and transnational corporations worked, and Allende was violently overthrown and killed. And, once the coup in Chile took place, the United States continued to support the Pinochet regime, including Manuel Contereras, who served as an agent of the CIA from 1974 to 1977, and went on to head Chile's intelligence agency, known as the DINA, which played the key role in the human rights abuses carried out in Chile.[261] The CIA concedes that its friend Contereras "became notorious for his involvement in human rights abuses," and had a key role in the car-bombing of former Chilean Ambassador to Washington Orlando Letelier and his young American assistant Ronnie Moffitt in the middle of Washington, D.C., in 1976.

As Eduardo Galeano wrote of Letelier in his later edition of *Open Veins of Latin America*—a book originally published in 1970 on the hopeful note of Allende's election in Chile (emphasis in text):

> In August of 1976, Orlando Letelier published an article describing the terror of the Pinochet dictatorship and the "economic liberty" of small privileged groups as two sides of the same coin. Letelier, who had been a minister in Salvador Allende's government, was exiled in the United States. There he was blown to pieces shortly afterwards. . . . Letelier described the massive destruction of gains made by the Chilean people during the Popular Unity government [of Salvador Allende]. The dictatorship had returned to their former owners half of the industrial monopolies and oligopolies which Allende nationalized, and put the other half up for sale. Firestone had bought the national tire factory, Parsons and Whittemore, a big paper plant. The Chilean economy, wrote Letelier, is more concentrated and monopolized now than on the eve of the Allende government. *Business free as never before, people in jail as never before; in Latin America free enterprise is incompatible with civil liberties.* . . .
>
> Infant mortality, substantially reduced during the Popular Unity regime, rose dramatically with Pinochet. When Letelier

was assassinated in a Washington street, one quarter of Chile's population was getting no income and survived thanks to foreign charity or their own stubbornness and guile.[262]

The nadir of Pinochet's reign was the bizarre state-within-a-state, Colonia Dignidad, a fascist German colony founded by Paul Schaefer, a Nazi and former medic of the Nazi's Luftwaffe.[263] Colonia Dignidad became a "clandestine detention and torture center" for the Pinochet regime. As one victim of the Colonia's torture explains, "Right after the coup, the Chilean military didn't know how to torture . . . . People would die very quickly. Germans in the colony knew how to keep a person alive for several days or weeks while putting him through the most terrible agony and humiliation."

But it was not enough for Pinochet and his US overlords to terrorize the Chilean population and to take from them all that had been given to them by their president, and then some. No, what was needed was to make sure that they would not even dare to rise up again to claim what was rightfully theirs. For this, all hope had to be extinguished.

And so, nine members of the Chilean military captured world-famous folk singer Victor Jara—Chile's Bob Dylan (or maybe Dylan was the US Victor Jara)—the day after the overthrow of Allende.[267] They took the forty-year-old, strikingly handsome Jara to the soccer stadium where they were holding, and in many cases torturing, five thousand other Chilean patriots, and tortured him in front of the other prisoners. As they smashed Jara's fingers with their gun butts, they told him that he would never play the guitar again. They eventually killed him and threw him out into the street, where he was found later with forty-four bullet wounds. This brutal murder was carried out not only to silence Jara's voice forever, but to demoralize the millions in Chile and around the world who found hope and solace in that voice.

It now appears that Pinochet's forces may also have murdered Pablo Neruda, Chile's poet laureate and winner of the Nobel Prize for literature, less than two weeks after the coup. While the cause of his death was initially listed as cancer, sixteen experts who examined his body after exhumation concluded that this was definitely not the cause of death.[265]

And the possibility of murder is raised by surrounding circumstances, including the fact that former Chilean President Eduardo Frei—remember the guy whose candidacy the US bankrolled throughout the 1960s?—was in fact murdered by lethal injection by Pinochet's forces in the same room of the same hospital where Neruda had died years before.[266] Sadly for Frei, he just had too much commitment to Chile's Constitutional order for the taste of Pinochet and the CIA. Indeed, the CIA had disparaged him in the past for his "unwillingness to betray Chile's long-standing tradition of civil, constitutional rule," referring to him as "a man 'with no pants on.'"[267] Apparently, only real men are willing to commit high treason against their own democratic country.

To further destroy the will of the Chilean people, the new regime engaged in the kidnapping of children from dissidents. Thousands of these children, many sent to other countries for adoption, never saw their parents again. Indeed, as I was writing this chapter, a news story popped up on my Facebook feed about a currently evolving scandal in Sweden.[268] Authorities there have recently discovered that hundreds of children brought to Sweden from Chile during the Pinochet years (1973 to 1992) were most likely stolen from their parents. One adoption agency in particular, Adoptionscentrum, is under investigation for trafficking at least 371 children, now adults of course, to Sweden during Pinochet's reign, all the while knowing that they had been forcibly taken from their parents. The president of Adoptionscentrum at the time in question is one of the leading candidates for prime minister, conservative politician Ulf Kristersson.

The Chilean coup had dire reverberations throughout the Southern Cone of South America, as the CIA itself recognizes. As it relates, "[w]ithin a year after the coup, the CIA and other US Government agencies were aware of bilateral cooperation among regional intelligence services to track the activities of and, in at least a few cases, kill political opponents. This was the precursor to Operation Condor, an intelligence-sharing arrangement among Chile, Argentina, Brazil, Paraguay and Uruguay established in 1975."

More than a "few" political opponents were killed by these regimes under Operation Condor, some of them, as in the case of Argentina, openly Nazi. As journalist Ben Norton explains, anywhere between sixty thousand to eighty thousand people were either killed or disappeared in Operation Condor which grew out of the Chilean coup.[269]

9

HONDURAS (2009)

THE US HAS BEEN INTERVENING IN, and indeed dominating, Honduras' internal affairs since the 1890s. Indeed, Honduras was the original "banana republic"—that is, a country which, by hook and by crook, "'became a foreign-controlled enclave that systematically swung the whole of Honduras into a one-crop [banana] economy whose wealth was carried off to New Orleans, New York, and later Boston.'"[270] What this meant for the Honduran people was disaster. US banana interests took over so much land—almost one million acres by 1914—that "Honduran peasants 'had no hope of access to their nation's good soil.'"[271]

To maintain the domination over Honduras and its economy, the US played a major part in developing the Honduran military which, by the mid-1960s, "had become . . . the country's 'most developed political institution' . . . ."[272] The US has used the Honduran military, as well as the huge military bases it has placed there, to dominate the rest of the region. Most notably, President Ronald Reagan used Honduras as the staging ground for the Contra War against Nicaragua in the 1980s. All of this has "greatly strengthened the militarization of Honduran society," and has led, in turn, to greater political repression in the form of "political assassinations, 'disappearances' and illegal detentions."[273]

It is against this backdrop that one of the crueler US interventions, this one under the "liberal" Obama administration, took place. This was the 2009 coup which deposed democratically elected Honduran President Manuel Zelaya. As the AP reported at the time, "Honduran President Manuel Zelaya was ousted in a military coup after betraying his own kind: a small clique of families that dominates the economy."[274] Zelaya's biggest sin was to have raised the minimum wage by 60 percent, infuriating business elites, both domestic and foreign (including, of course, Chiquita Banana).

Given such audacious crimes, Zelaya had to be gotten rid of. And so, the Honduran military took the direct route, kidnapping Zelaya at gunpoint in the middle of the night and flying him out of the country to Costa Rica while he was still in his pajamas.

Not surprisingly, the two key military generals who carried out this coup were trained by the US at its infamous US Army School of the Americas (SOA), now located in Columbus, Georgia, and now known as the Western Hemisphere Institute for Security Cooperation (WHINSEC). WHINSEC trained over five hundred Honduran officers from 2001 through 2009, and the general who violently kidnapped Zelaya (Romeo Orlando Vásquez Velásquez) is a two-time graduate.[275] Gen. Luis Javier Prince Suazo, the head of the Honduran Air Force, who arranged to have Zelaya flown into exile, was also trained at the School of the Americas.

I say it is not surprising that the coup leaders were trained by the US, for as an academic named Jonathan Caverley, an associate professor at the Naval War College, concluded in a 2015 working paper, there is a direct link between US military training of foreign troops and "an increased likelihood of military coups."[276]

Meanwhile, more details have recently emerged that show an even closer connection between the US and the coup than once previously known. As a 2017 exposé in *The Intercept* explains, "[h]idden actors during the crisis tilted Honduras toward chaos, undermined official US policy after the coup, and ushered in a new era of militarization that has left a trail of violence and repression in its wake."[277]

In the words of Martin Edwin Andersen—former communications director for the Center for Hemispheric Defense Studies (CHDS) at the US Southern Command who later turned whistleblower—"some of my senior colleagues at US Southern Command should have been punished for their hands-on role in the coup. To the best of my knowledge none were, even as Honduras now crashes and burns as the most violent country in the Western Hemisphere."[278] Andersen goes on to state that, [i]n fact, perhaps still unbeknownst to the State Department, part of the real-time coup quarterbacking occurred just blocks from Capitol."

What we now know is that the US and Honduran military officers and diplomats, who generally tend to be thick as thieves, partied together the night before the coup at the house of the US Embassy's defense attaché, Andrew Papp. The very next morning, soldiers kidnapped President Zelaya, brought him to Soto Cano, the huge military base which is shared jointly by US and Honduran forces, and then flew him from there out of the country to Costa Rica. While the US military officials at the base claim that they never knew Zelaya was there or that he was flown out of the base, this seems highly unlikely given the fact that (1) the US ambassador was fully aware of the coup by this time; and (2) the Honduran military does not do anything without US approval, especially at the Soto Cano base—the biggest US military base in the region.

In addition, in the months leading up to the coup, the NED—the Reagan-era organization created to use "soft power" to meddle in other country's affairs and even help foment regime change—provided $1.2 million to the International Republican Institute to organize against Zelaya and his reforms, and to support the opposition groups which ended up toppling him.[279]

And, once Zelaya was successfully ousted, the US, and in particular the Pentagon and then–Secretary of State Hillary Clinton, made sure that he stayed gone. The Center for Economic and Policy Research explains,[280] "the Pentagon's main interest was in maintaining relations with a close military ally, rather than in overturning the coup. Though the battle over Honduras appeared to be fought along partisan lines, in the end it was the Obama administration's State Department that sabotaged efforts to have Zelaya restored to the presidency, as statements by former Secretary Clinton and other high-level officials admit."

For example, as the *National Catholic Reporter* wrote at the time, while "[t]he Foreign Operations Appropriations Act requires that US military aid and training be suspended when a country undergoes a military coup, and the Obama administration has indicated those steps have been taken," those steps in fact were never taken.

Indeed, as the *NCR* article points out, I, along with Father Roy Bourgeois and other supporters of SOA Watch, personally would witness firsthand the falsehood of Obama's claim when we traveled to Honduras days after the coup.

Our first stop on this trip was to visit the US's Soto Cano Air Base where the US Southern Command's Joint Task Force-Bravo is stationed. The base was humming with activity, seemingly unaffected by the coup which had just happened, and we asked a Sgt. Reyes at the base point blank whether it was true that the US military had halted its joint operations with the Colombian military post-coup. Reyes responded, and I took notes of this at the time, that the US relationship with the Honduran military after the coup was "stable. Nothing has changed. That's just something they're telling the press." In addition, Lee Rials, public affairs officer for WHINSEC, confirmed post-coup that Honduran officers were still being trained at WHINSEC.

As diplomatic cables later obtained through a FOIA request revealed, it turns out that while the US announced on July 1, 2009, that it had "'cut off contact with those who have conducted the coup,'" Secretary of State Clinton secretly countermanded that order the very next day by writing to the US Embassy and "giving approval to 'engage elements of the Honduran Armed Forces and de facto regime'. . . ."[281]

Meanwhile, Col. Andrew Papp, the defense attaché who hosted the party the night before the coup, made it clear to the Honduran military that "we still wanted a relationship when this was all done with" regardless of whether the coup were reversed or not.[282]

For its part, the CHDS in Washington, D.C. met with Honduran military leaders shortly after the coup and apparently gave them a pat on the back for their overthrow of Zelaya on the basis that, in its view, "they prevented socialism from coming 'to the borders of the United States.'" Whistleblower Martin Edwin Andersen explains, in quite colorful terms: "Within days I found that another senior (and far-right) CHDS staff member, a vicious and vocal critic of Obama, and his minions had coordinated meetings for uniformed Honduran coup representatives on Capitol Hill, including the office of at least one now-retired Senator, and other places in our nation's capital, even as deadly 'mop up' operations took place in Tegucigalpa and in the countryside."

In addition, CHDS Director Richard Downie later sent a memo to the Department of Defense and State Department saying, in effect, "that the US wouldn't want to push Zelaya back into office and so it would give the coup government some time to set things up before moving on to elections."

Downie later explained, "'that's what ended up happening'"—that is, the coup government moved on with elections without Zelaya having been returned to power and without Zelaya on the ballot. And it was discovered later how this came

to be. Thus, recently declassified US military intelligence documents show that while the official position of the US government
had been that no elections should go forward without Zelaya,
US SOUTHCOM was actually encouraging the coup government to do just that—to hold on until new elections were held in
the absence of Zelaya. The coup government took this as its cue
and ran with it.

As we would find out later in Hillary Clinton's vanity book,
Hard Choices, she too had proudly worked behind the scenes to
ensure that elections would go forward in Honduras after the
coup swiftly, without Zelaya, and in such a way as to "render
the question of Zelaya moot." Quite tellingly, Clinton would
later excise the above-quoted passage from her book when the
paperback edition came out,[283] after she was shocked to realize
that people were inexplicably upset by her cynical maneuvers to
undermine democracy in Honduras.

One way that the Clinton State Department maneuvered to
keep Zelaya from regaining office was to declare in September
of 2009 that that his ouster from power did not constitute a coup
requiring the cutting off military assistance.[284] This declaration
was made against all evidence to the contrary and in contradiction of the US Embassy's earlier conclusion in June that it was an
"'open and shut'" case that what happened was an "'illegal and
unconstitutional coup.'"[285]

In addition, the State Department went ahead and announced
even before elections were held that the US would recognize
them even without Zelaya.[286] As *The Intercept* notes, US officials
even went so far as to block a resolution at the Organization of
American States that called for the restoration of Zelaya to office
before elections were held.

The reader might also recall that a key public relations
spokesman for the new coup regime was none other than Clinton
campaign team member Lanny Davis.[287]

Ultimately, the US stood nearly alone in the Western Hemisphere in recognizing the election of President Porfirio Lobo Sosa that followed the coup, though this election took place in the absence of Zelaya being returned to Honduras and able to participate in the election. Dana Frank, writing in the *New York Times*, explained the significance of this:

> President Obama quickly recognized Mr. Lobo's victory, even when most of Latin America would not. Mr. Lobo's government is, in fact, a child of the coup. It retains most of the military figures who perpetrated the coup, and no one has gone to jail for starting it.
>
> This chain of events—a coup that the United States didn't stop, a fraudulent election that it accepted—has now allowed corruption to mushroom. The judicial system hardly functions. Impunity reigns. At least 34 members of the opposition have disappeared or been killed, and more than 300 people have been killed by state security forces since the coup, according to the leading human rights organization COFADEH. At least 13 journalists have been killed since Mr. Lobo took office, according to the Committee to Protect Journalists.

Frank, citing a report by the Fellowship of Reconciliation, noted that, "[s]ince the coup the United States has maintained and in some areas increased military and police financing for Honduras and has been enlarging its military bases there . . . ."[288]

One individual who took umbrage at the pro-coup machinations of people like Hillary Clinton was Honduran Berta Cáceras, the acclaimed environmental and human right activist, who was murdered by members of the Honduran Special Forces in 2016. As Berta was quoted as saying shortly before her death, "We're coming out of a coup that we can't put behind us. We can't reverse it. It just kept going. And after, there was the issue of the elections. The same Hillary Clinton, in her book, *Hard Choices*, practically said what was going to happen in Honduras. This demonstrates the meddling of North Americans in our country."[289]

Clinton was responsible for Berta's plight in one other significant way. Thus, Clinton's State Department year after year certified that the Honduras military was in compliance with US human rights criteria, despite its violent persecution of activists, thereby allowing military aid to be freed up for Honduras. The State Department did so even the year that Berta was murdered.[290]

And, it has been revealed that, not too surprisingly, the Special Forces who actually killed Berta were themselves trained by the US. As *The Guardian* recently reported:

> Leaked court documents raise concerns that the murder of the Honduran environmentalist Berta Cáceres was an extrajudicial killing planned by military intelligence specialists linked to the country's US–trained special forces, a Guardian investigation can reveal.
>
> A legal source close to the investigation told the Guardian: "The murder of Berta Cáceres has all the characteristics of a well-planned operation designed by military intelligence, where it is absolutely normal to contract civilians as assassins."[291]

To this day, the US remains closely allied to Honduras, continuing to use it as a giant military base from which to project its power throughout the region. Indeed, Honduras has once been described as "USS Honduras"—"a stationary, unsinkable aircraft carrier, strategically anchored" in the middle of Latin America.[292] And, the terrible repression unleashed by the 2009 coup continues at the hands of a military the US continues to support. Indeed, as CEPR explains, "[s]ince the coup, the militarization of Honduras has increased. While human rights abuses continue to shock the public, US security assistance and military training continue unabated."

As Latin American specialist Greg Grandin recently explained, "hundreds of peasant activists and indigenous activists have been killed. Scores of gay rights activists have been killed . . . . [I]t's just a nightmare in Honduras. . . . And Berta Cáceres, in that interview, says what was installed after the coup was something like a permanent counterinsurgency on behalf of transnational capital. And that was—that wouldn't have been possible if it were not for Hillary Clinton's normalization of that election, or legitimacy."293

In addition, Honduras is the most dangerous country in the Hemisphere to be a journalist, with scores of journalists killed since the 2009 coup.294 Moreover, as has recently been reported, the Garifunas—Hondurans of African descent who have been there for centuries—are being subjected to intense discrimination and are being forced off their land in large numbers by real estate developers and others who covet their land, with many being forced to leave Honduras altogether.295

And all of this post-coup repression was not accidental, but was in fact part of the plan for those in Washington who supported the coup. As whistleblower Martin Edwin Andersen explained in a sworn affidavit, there was not only "involvement in the Honduran coup" by senior colleagues at Southern Command Key, but also "behind the scenes advocacy of death squads by people who literally met privately with hundreds of active-duty Latin American military officers each year . . . ." He goes on to explain that this revelation "was accompanied by my discovery that another CHDS colleague had worked for [Chilean Dictator Augusto] Pinochet's DINA death squad operation. It was DINA that had killed an exiled foreign minister, Orlando Letelier, and his American assistant, Ronni Moffitt, in a car bombing near the White House, one of the gravest terrorist attacks in our nation's capital before 9/11."

Andersen ends his affidavit with the following question: "Are not the clandestine and unpunished involvement in the Honduran coup, as well as the promotion of torture and murder, challenges to the rule of law as well as fundamental American values?" Sadly, history has shown that the answer to this question is a resounding no.

10

NICARAGUA

THE US HAS BEEN MEDDLING IN Nicaragua for well over 150
years, treating it like its own vassal state. The first foray came
in the 1850s, when William Walker went to Central America to
liberate the region as only a God-fearing white man could. As
Eduardo Galeano wrote in his opus, *Open Veins of Latin America*:

> In the geopolitical concept of imperialism, Central America is
> no more than a natural appendage of the United States. Not
> even Abraham Lincoln, who also contemplated annexation,
> could resist the 'manifest destiny' of the great power to dictate
> to contiguous areas.
>
> In the middle of the nineteenth century the filibusterer
> William Walker, operating on behalf of bankers Morgan and
> Garrison, invaded Central America at the head of a band of
> assassins. With the obliging support of the US government,
> Walker robbed, killed, burned, and in successive expeditions
> proclaimed himself president of Nicaragua, El Salvador, and
> Honduras. He restored slavery in the areas that suffered his
> devastating occupation, thus continuing his country's phil-
> anthropic work in the states that had just been seized from
> Mexico. He was welcomed back to the United States a national
> hero. From then on, invasions, interventions, bombardments,

forced loans, and gun-point treaties followed one after the other.

One big reason the United States never relented from its attempt to control Nicaragua, a country with both a Pacific and Atlantic coast, was its huge lake (Lake Nicaragua) which could be transformed into a canal for shipping much larger than the Panama Canal. Indeed, in 1914, the United States bought the rights to build this canal for $3 million. This $3 million also bought them the leasing rights to two Nicaraguan islands as well as the right to build a naval base in the Gulf of Fonseca.

The problem was that the Nicaraguans are a quite proud and independent people, and they bristled over the United States' attempts to control their country. The Nicaraguans would therefore rise up in protest often against US intervention. In response, the United States began militarily intervening in Nicaragua in 1912, sending in the Marines periodically to quell opposition. However, every time the Marines would withdraw, the people would rise up again. And so, in 1927, the Marines began to occupy Nicaragua.

Not too surprisingly, the Nicaraguans were quite unhappy about the presence of foreign troops on their soil and about being declared a "protectorate of the United States."

One brave Nicaraguan, Augusto Cesar Sandino, organized a band of guerillas to attack and molest the Marines, and he was quite successful in doing so. Indeed, Sandino would lead about five hundred attacks on the Marines who were never able to defeat Sandino or to even find where he and his band of merry men were hiding.

In 1933, the United States, now really desperate, would try out some of the world's first aerial bombings against Sandino's guerillas as well as the sympathetic, rural Nicaraguan population. Notwithstanding the United States' much superior firepower, Sandino and his forces would successfully oust the Marines in 1934. However, before leaving Nicaragua, the US Marines helped to set up the brutal National Guard (*Guardia Nacional*) to maintain order in Nicaragua in their stead. The United States installed a man named Anastasio Somoza Garcia as the head of the National Guard in 1934.

Unable to defeat Sandino, Somoza lured Sandino to the capital, Managua, with the promise of a peace accord and had him assassinated. In 1936, with Sandino out of the way, Anastasio Somoza Garcia, with the full backing of the United States, became the dictatorial ruler of Nicaragua. It was of Somoza that President Roosevelt remarked, "He is a son of a bitch, but he's our son of a bitch." With the strong backing of the United States, Anastasio Somoza Garcia, his son, and then his grandson would rule Nicaragua with an iron hand continuously until the 1979 Revolution.

However, Somoza would not go down easily, and the dictatorship indeed showed us its worst brutality in its final death throes. The US was of course more than willing to lend a hand to help Somoza violently cling to power. As Noam Chomsky so well explains in his book, *What Uncle Sam Really Wants*:

> When his rule was challenged by the Sandinistas [the insurgent group named after Augusto Cesar Sandino] in the late 1970s, the US first tried to institute what was called "Somocismo [Somoza-ism] without Somoza"-that is, the whole corrupt system intact, but with somebody else at the top. That didn't work, so President Carter tried to maintain Somoza's National Guard as a base for US power.
>
> The National Guard had always been remarkably brutal and sadistic. By June 1979, it was carrying out massive atrocities in the war against the Sandinistas, bombing residential neighborhoods in Managua, killing tens of thousands of people. At that point, the US ambassador sent a cable to the White House saying it would be "ill advised" to tell the Guard to call

off the bombing, because that might interfere with the policy of keeping them in power and the Sandinistas out.

Our ambassador to the Organization of American States also spoke in favor of "Somocismo without Somoza," but the OAS rejected the suggestion flat out. A few days later, Somoza flew off to Miami with what was left of the Nicaraguan national treasury, and the Guard collapsed.

The Carter administration flew Guard commanders out of the country in planes with Red Cross markings (a war crime), and began to reconstitute the Guard on Nicaragua's borders. They also used Argentina as a proxy. (At that time, Argentina was under the rule of neo-Nazi generals, but they took a little time off from torturing and murdering their own population to help reestablish the Guard-soon to be renamed the contras, or "freedom fighters.")

Unable to forgive the Nicaraguans for ousting one of their beloved dictators, just as it could not forgive the Iranians for the same offense, the United States would then back these Contra forces throughout the 1980s.

While Ronald Reagan would refer to the Contras as the "moral equivalent of our Founding Fathers," this did not reflect so well on our Founding Fathers. For example, an *LA Times* article from 1985 cited the International Human Rights Law Group who documented "a pattern of brutality against largely unarmed civilians, including rape, torture, kidnappings, mutilation and other abuses" by the Contra forces.

As just one example of this, the *LA Times* related the following account:

Children Slain
Typical among them was an Oct. 28, 1982, contra attack on the rural area of El Jicaro in northern Nicaragua. In an affidavit,

Maria Bustillo, 57, testified that five armed men dressed in the
FDN's blue uniforms burst into her house and dragged away
her husband Ricardo, a Roman Catholic activist, and five of
their children. The next morning she found the mutilated bodies of the children. Her husband's body was found later.[296]

In addition to funding and training the Contras, the United
States would also mine Nicaragua's harbors. And, the United
States did so without even informing its allies who regularly
anchored there. The International Court of Justice (ICJ) later
found in the case of *Nicaragua v. United States* (1986), that because
"neither before the laying of the mines, nor subsequently, did the
United States government issue any public and official warning
to international shipping of the existence and location of the
mines . . . vessels of the Dutch, Panamanian, Soviet, Liberian and
Japanese registry . . . were damaged by the mines. . . ." The ICJ,
which concluded that President Reagan had personally ordered
this mining operation, found the callousness of the United States
toward such third-party countries particularly reprehensible.

The ICJ found that the United States violated international
law in its bilateral treaties with Nicaragua through the mining of
the harbors, various other terrorist attacks such as the destruction
of Nicaragua's oil storage facilities and pipelines, and through
the funding and training of the Contras. As for the training, the
ICJ, based upon the affidavit of Contra leader Edgar Chamorro,
found that "training was at the outset provided by [fascist]
Argentine military officers, paid by the CIA, gradually replaced
by CIA personnel" who took over the training themselves.

According to Chamorro, the CIA trained the Contras in
"guerilla warfare, sabotage, demolitions, and in the use of a vari-
ety of weapons. . . ." Chamorro described the CIA officials as
more than advisers to the Contras. Rather, they were the leaders of the group, with Chamorro attributing "virtually a power

of command to the CIA operatives." The ICJ found that, under the CIA's direction and control, the Contras carried out numerous incidents of "kidnapping, assassinations, torture, rape, killing of prisoners, and killing of civilians not dictated by military necessity."

In addition, the ICJ found that the United States violated international law norms through the CIA's *Psychological Operations in Guerilla Warfare* manual which, among other things, advised the Contra forces to organize people for public executions. Specifically, the manual called for "Selective Use of Violence for Propagandistic Effects" in which "selected and planned targets, such as court judges, *mesta* judges, police and State Security officials, CDS chiefs, etc." would be "neutralize[d]" by a particular population which "will be present, [and] take part in the act" of killing the target.

The United States not only disregarded the ICJ's judgment—pursuant to which Nicaragua estimated it was owed nearly $400 million in compensation—but also declared that it was no longer subject to ICJ jurisdiction at all unless it explicitly consented to such for a particular case. Justice is, after all, to be administered against the weak, not the strong.

Moreover, the atrocities of the Contras became such a problem that the US Congress ended up suspending their funding through legislation known as the Boland Amendment. Undeterred, the Reagan administration found creative ways to continue arming and bankrolling the Contras, nonetheless.

In addition to funding the Contras through illicit sales of cocaine, with at least $14 million in drug sales being used as seed money to fund the post-Boland Amendment arms trade to the Contras,[297] the Reagan administration would also turn to Iran to aid his scheme. The problem there was that the United States was then supporting Iraq in its war against Iran, and there was therefore an arms embargo against Iran at this time. Again, Reagan would find a way. As we would learn later through what would come to be known as the Iran-Contra Scandal, Reagan would have the CIA secretly sell Iran more than 1,500 TOW missiles in return for $30 million—$18 million of which would go to the Contras.[298] Here is another example of where the US's covert interference in other countries subverted our own democracy as well.

Meanwhile, nothing but total capitulation by the Sandinistas would suffice for Reagan. Thus, as the ICJ related, revolutionary leader and then–Nicaraguan president, Daniel Ortega, made it clear that he would give into all of Reagan's stated demands (i.e., that he would send home the Cuban and Russians advisers and not support the FMLN guerillas in El Salvador) in return for only "one thing: that they don't attack us, that the United States stop arming and financing . . . the gangs that kill our people, burn our crops and force us to divert enormous human and economic resources into war when we desperately need them for development." But Reagan would not relent until the Sandinistas and Ortega were out of power altogether.

Meanwhile, even in the midst of Reagan's brutal Contra War, the Sandinistas created democracy in Nicaragua for the first time in its history. As Professor Ricardo Perez explains, "[t]he democracy that was built under the FSLN is a democracy for the great majority of Nicaraguans and not a democracy for a few. Under the low-intensity war promoted and sustained by the United States in 1984, the first multi-party elections outside the will of the United States took place for the first time in Nicaraguan history when they decided who would govern Nicaragua."[299]

And then, as Professor Perez further explains, it was Daniel Ortega who helped bring peace and reconciliation to the country through the Peace Agreements of Esquipulas and Sapoá, pursuant to which he stood for elections nine months early, and stepped down when he lost the vote in 1989. As Perez explains, Ortega took such steps "to stop and put an end to the unjust war imposed by the United States and therefore to lead to the construction of peace and strengthen democracy, which until then lacked a culture of peace and democracy in Nicaragua."

The US actually ramped up the Contra terror war against Nicaragua until the eve of the 1990 election, and it made it clear to the Nicaraguan people that the war would continue unless the elections went the right way—that is, if Ortega were voted out of office. However, the US did not stop with this blatant extortion to secure the election outcome it so desired. Thus, according to the *Oxford Journal* study, the US engaged in overt election meddling, along with a covert component, to get the job done.

The US's machinations were well explained by a group of US military veterans turned peace activists, who went to Nicaragua to observe the run-up to the elections and their aftermath. In their report, they detailed the three pillars of the US's election meddling campaign:

> President Bush continued the US economic embargo against Nicaragua by again declaring on October 25, 1989, that Nicaragua posed an "unusual and extraordinary threat to the national security and foreign policy of the United States." The economic situation throughout Nicaragua continues to force the majority of people to live in painful depravity.
>
> The US Congress and the CIA have combined to finance, with what are believed to be unprecedented amounts of money, the so-called opposition political parties in an effort to defeat the majority Sandinista Party in the February 1990 elections.
>
> In effect, the US orchestrated and financed 3-pronged attack through use of "low intensity" warfare against Nicaragua is in full force: (1) continued Contra terrorism throughout Nicaragua's rural areas, (2) continued economic strangulation, and (3) unprecedented efforts to purchase the internal political process and elections.[300]

As for the first prong of the US campaign, the report explains that Congress appropriated new funding for the Contras in April of 1989, and the funding was authorized at least until just after the February 1990 elections—again, this would depend on the outcome. Lest there were any doubt as to the intentions of the timing of this aid package, "[t]he Contras are communicating to virtually all rural campesinos, through word of mouth, distribution of US funded leaflets, and direct threats, that they will 'make the war worse than ever if the FSLN wins the elections.' Dr. Summerfield [an English psychiatrist studying the effects of the Contra war on the Nicaraguan population] suggested that a lot of people may not vote because of the fear of terrorist reprisals, like murder and maiming."

As for the second prong of the election intervention, President Bush went "on record saying he would lift the embargo if Violeta Chomorro, Presidential candidate for UNO, is elected" over Daniel Ortega.

Finally, as for the actual purchasing of the election, according to S. Brian Willson—the Vietnam veteran who famously lost his legs sitting in on train tracks to stop armaments from being shipped from the US to the war in Central America and who currently lives in Grenada, Nicaragua—the CIA and NED combined to provide nearly $50 million, or around $14 per each eligible voter in Nicaragua, to support the opposition groups in Nicaragua.[301]

Not surprisingly, the Nicaraguans succumbed to this combination of terror, economic pressure, and direct interference in the political process, and voted out Daniel Ortega in the 1990 elections. Ironically, the 1990 Nicaraguan elections are widely considered in the US to be Nicaragua's first democratic elections, when they were anything but. However, notwithstanding the blatant interference of the US on the side opposing him, Daniel Ortega willingly stepped down as president, allowing peace, if an uneasy one, to finally come to Nicaragua after ten years of US-sponsored war.[302]

The US has continued its interference in Nicaragua's elections and political life. For example, in the 2001 elections—elections in which I served as an international observer—the US blatantly threatened again that a Sandinista victory could lead to both a cessation of US aid to Nicaragua as well as a return to the US's "oppositional policies" of the 1980s, a not-so-veiled threat of the restart of the Contra War.[303]

This sort of blackmail is a common tactic of the US to sway elections, and was used effectively, if not cruelly, against the left-ist candidate of El Salvador during the 2004 presidential election campaign. As William Blum explains:

Washington's target in this election was Schafik Handal, candidate of the FMLN, the leftist former guerrilla group. He said he would withdraw El Salvador's 380 troops from Iraq as well as reviewing other pro-US policies; he would also take another look at the privatizations of Salvadoran industries, and would reinstate diplomatic relations with Cuba. His opponent was Tony Saca of the incumbent Arena Party, a pro-US, pro-free market organization of the extreme right, which in the bloody civil war days had featured death squads and the infamous assassination of Archbishop Oscar Romero.

During a February visit to the country, the US Assistant Secretary of State for Western Hemisphere Affairs, met with all the presidential candidates except Handal. He warned of possible repercussions in US-Salvadoran relations if Handal were elected. Three Republican congressmen threatened to block the renewal of annual work visas for some 300,000 Salvadorans in the United States if El Salvador opted for the FMLN. And Congressman Thomas Tancredo of Colorado stated that if the

FMLN won, "it could mean a radical change" in US policy on remittances to El Salvador.

Washington's attitude was exploited by Arena and the generally conservative Salvadoran press, who mounted a scare campaign, and it became widely believed that a Handal victory could result in mass deportations of Salvadorans from the United States and a drop in remittances. Arena won the election with about 57 percent of the vote to some 36 percent for the FMLN.[304]

Meanwhile, during the 2001 Nicaraguan elections, the US Ambassador, Oliver Garza, even went so far as to join right-wing candidate Enrique Bolaños on the campaign trail where he proceeded to give out food to those attending Bolaños' events. That is, "[t]he US ambassador literally campaigned for Ortega's opponent, Enrique Bolaños. A senior analyst in Nicaragua for Gallup, the international pollsters, was moved to declare: '[n]ever in my whole life have I seen a sitting ambassador get publicly involved in a sovereign country's electoral process, nor have I ever heard of it.'"[305]

With such help, Bolaños came out on top, despite the fact that the Sandinistas were ahead in the polls leading up to the time of the election.[306]

Against great odds, the Sandinistas would be voted back into power in 2006, and they remain the governing party to this day, with Daniel Ortega as president. And, with victory came great advances for the Nicaraguan people.

Luca Di Fabio, writing quite recently for the anti-poverty NGO, The Borgen Project, explained that "[t]he amount of economic growth in Nicaragua is an unusual and unprecedented phenomenon in the Central American peninsula," and that "[e]xperts argue that such improvements in economic growth in Nicaragua are largely attributable to the re-election of President

Daniel Ortega" who led the country to annual economic growth of nearly 5 percent every year since 2011, and who helped reduce poverty in Nicaragua by 30 percent.[307]

The independent Latin American Geopolitical Strategic Center (CELAG) further explains how Ortega successfully took Nicaragua down a different path than his neighbors, leading to a more prosperous, stable, and peaceful country. As CELAG concludes:

> It should be said that Nicaragua has important differences with neighbors such as Honduras, Guatemala and even El Salvador, countries that after the Peace Accords were prosecuted towards violent neoliberalism through various initiatives, mostly sponsored by the US government-private sector (read, for example, the Initiative for the Security of Central America and the Alliance for Prosperity). Within the framework of these plans, there has been a growing militarization and an upsurge of violence, in the style of Plan Colombia.
>
> Unlike these trajectories, Nicaragua shows (with the limitations and contradictions that must be pointed out) economic growth and poverty reduction, its security indices are infinitely greater than those of the countries of the Northern Triangle and its residents have not had to flee to the US border in search of better lives in the same proportion as Salvadorans, Guatemalans and Hondurans have done it. . . .[308]

And so again, we see Ortega continuing to bring peace and stability to Nicaragua. The result was that, as of October of 2017, he had nearly an 80 percent approval rating.[309] Moreover, in 2017, Nicaragua polled the highest in all of Latin America on the issue of whether the government was leading in the interests of all of the people, and it polled second on the overall evaluation of the functioning of its democracy.[310]

The US could not sit idly by as a political movement it had spent millions to destroy was demonstrating such seemingly impossible success. It had to destroy this "danger of a good example," in the word of Noam Chomsky. It seized upon the opportunity presented by demonstrations against Ortega's announcement of very modest social security reforms on April 16, 2018, to spring its forces into action. The US and its allies in Nicaragua would run the same game plan run in so many other attempts at regime change—to create violent provocations which would lead to a reaction by the state which then could be blamed for the ensuing chaos. The plan worked like a charm, at least for three terrifying months.

The independent Nicaraguan media collective, Tortilla Con Sal, summarized the initial moves of what the Nicaraguan government is now portraying as a "soft coup":

> During the days 19, 20 and 21 of April the armed groups of the political opposition mixed with students and young people and also integrated hundreds of delinquents recruited of different cities with the purpose of intensifying the attacks. They attacked all kinds of infrastructure with firearms, spell weapons and Molotov cocktails. Since its inception, the protests have been very violent. Nevertheless, an image of disproportionate repression and even speech of "massacres" has been projected by means of a tremendous machinery of disinformation in the social networks and the news media of the private company and its international allies. An important component of misinformation has been the manipulation of the figures of the dead and wounded.[311]

And, as the days passed, the brutality and violence of the extreme opposition groups only increased. This violence greatly resembled that of the Contras in the 1980s. John Perry, an American living in Masaya, Nicaragua—the eye of the storm during this period—detailed the violence which he and his Nicaraguan wife witnessed firsthand:

> In the first [phase of the protests], barricades that had been removed were re-erected, again blocking streets, with Masaya again the most affected. The "peaceful" protesters armed themselves with homemade mortars, repelling attempts by the police or Sandinista supporters to regain control. Rival marches took place, in many cases without problems, but friends of mine took part in a "peace" march that was greeted by hails of stones and mortar fire. A wave of destruction began, focusing first on Sandinista offices, then moving on to public buildings, including town halls and in some cases schools and health centers. Houses of some Sandinista supporters in Masaya were ransacked or burned down. According to neighbors who witnessed it, alongside genuine protesters were unemployed youths paid $10–15 per night, some brought in by lorry, defending the barricades, attacking the police, and ransacking shops.[312]

And, while the Nicaraguan government, the subject of one of the wildest and deceptive media campaigns ever waged against a government, was being accused of using "genocidal" violence during this crisis, this is a characterization more applicable to the extreme opposition. As the *Morning Star* of the UK relates:

> A source in the city of Esteli told the Star: "Here in Esteli now the opposition are marking the houses of people identified as Sandinista.
>
> We're all taking what precautions we can, but I don't think the opposition are in the least interested in dialogue. They are determined not just to oust the government but to destroy the FSLN [Sandinista National Liberation Front]."[313]

I have heard such stories from a number of sources in Nicaragua who believe, as the witness does above, that the violent opposition is bent upon destroying the FSLN and indeed all memories of it, for example by destroying Sandinista memorials throughout Nicaragua.

Meanwhile, each Sandinista government employee and police officer killed is manipulatively placed in the tally of dead allegedly killed by the state. George Orwell could not conjure up a more dastardly tale of media manipulation.

And, of course, in the background of all of this is the United States which continues its efforts to unseat the Sandinistas who had the audacity to overthrow the US-backed dictator in 1979. As we learned from journalist Max Blumenthal, "a publication funded by the US government's regime change arm, the National Endowment for Democracy (NED), bluntly asserted that organizations backed by the NED have spent years and millions of dollars 'laying the groundwork for insurrection' in Nicaragua."[314] And, that groundwork bore the desired, bad fruit.

Meanwhile, the United States continues to punish Nicaragua, the most stable and prosperous country in Central America after successfully breaking off from US domination, for its impertinence in overthrowing the Somoza dictatorship, having the audacity to survive the Contra War which claimed fifty thousand lives, voting back in the Sandinistas, and for now working with the Chinese to build the canal that the United States has coveted for so long. Thus, as I write these lines, the US Senate is considering passage of the "Nica Act," already passed by the House, which would cut Nicaragua off from multilateral loans (e.g., from the World Bank, IMF). This, apparently, will show Nicaragua and other countries what they get for deciding to go their own way.

I leave this discussion with the conclusory words of CELAG which, though clearly quite critical of Daniel Ortega, expresses the proper concerns about the current events in Nicaragua:

What is happening in Nicaragua is of the utmost gravity. It is, together with Costa Rica, the only country in Central America that maintains political, economic, social and security lines that seek to go beyond neoliberal orthodoxy, albeit in a contradictory and ambivalent manner, in a region plunged in misery and violence. But, unlike Costa Rica, Nicaragua does it without bowing to the interests of US foreign policy. . . . [I]t is fundamental to consider the importance of Nicaragua in the regional geopolitics, the interests that may be at stake and the sectors that could be looking to destabilize the government of the day. This does not imply that there is no discontent in different sectors of society. But what is striking is the way in which this disagreement is channeled, the way in which it is being presented by the hegemonic press and the arguments that are raised as the main complaints or claims to the government. . . .

It is important to visualize, keep in mind, what happened in the countries that enjoyed "democratic springs" in the last decades: Who took power? What transformations were there? In favor of what sectors? What role did the USA play? Maybe after each spring 2.0 what is anticipated, more than a summer, is another long neoliberal winter without any obstacle or claim on the part of the international community.[315]

11

UKRAINE (2014)

FIRST OF ALL, LET'S START FROM the premise that there was an illegal *coup d'etat* in February 2014 which overthrew the democratically elected government of Viktor Yanukovych, a leader who was at least favorably disposed toward Russia. Indeed, in a moment of candor, George Friedman, the head of the private US intelligence firm Stratfor, an organization which prides itself on independent geopolitical analysis, agreed with Russian claims that the overthrow of Yanukovych was indeed a US-backed coup.

Mincing no words, Friedman told the Russian paper *Kommersant, "Russia calls the events that took place at the beginning of this year a coup d'etat organized by the United States. And it truly was the most blatant coup in history."* (emphasis added).[316] Friedman's assessment that the coup was motivated by the US's one-hundred-year obsession with preventing "any state to amass too much power in Europe." In light of this obsession, Friedman had predicted three years before the coup "that as soon as Russia starts to increase its power and demonstrate it, a crisis would occur in Ukraine," and that crisis would be made in the USA. And as history has shown, Friedman was right.

The ouster of Yanukovych, which came under the pressure from street protests, some violent, was prompted by his "offense"—or at least the press here considered it an offense—of reconsidering whether to enter an association agreement with the European Union in light of a pretty decent deal being offered from Vladimir Putin to stay economically integrated with Russia—a deal which included Russia buying $15 billion of Ukrainian government bonds and cutting gas prices.[317]

For Yanukovych to at least consider the deal offered by Putin was not irrational, especially given that "[e]conomic experts [at the time] say Ukraine desperately needs at least $10b in the coming months to avoid bankruptcy."[318]

Moreover, it is fair to say that Ukraine was under a great deal of pressure from the West in the form of the US-dominated IMF which had approved a $15.1 billion loan for Ukraine in 2010 and then suspended it, after only paying out $3 billion of the loan, in light of Ukraine's failure to pursue austerity measures, such as pension "reforms" (meaning cuts) and the increase of consumer gas prices.[319] And, the IMF would only approve a new loan deal on condition of Ukraine "drastically increasing the gas bills of Ukrainians while freezing salaries at the current level and doing additional budget cuts."[320] Indeed, Yanukovych's prime minister at the time cited the onerous requirements of the IMF loan then on the table as a big reason for backing out of the EU deal.[321] An IMF deal, by the way, ended up being approved very shortly after the coup which unseated Yanukovych.

In addition, buried within the EU deal were provisos that would have required Ukraine to submit to NATO military security policy, a controversial requirement indeed.[322] And, as it has turned out, Kiev's relationship with NATO deepened after the toppling of Yanukovych and after the new government entered the Association Agreement with the EU. As NATO gloated thereafter, "[w]e will continue to promote the development of greater interoperability between Ukrainian and NATO forces. NATO's enhanced advisory presence in Kyiv is already in place and will continue to grow. As requested by Ukraine, Allies will continue to provide expertise as Ukraine completes its comprehensive defense and security sector review. The comprehensive reform agenda undertaken by Ukraine in the context of its ANP [Annual National Program] with NATO, as well as in the context of its Association Agreement with the EU, will further strengthen Ukraine."[323]

As the *New York Times* acknowledged when the new president, Poroshenko, signed the EU Agreement, "[o]ne of Mr. Putin's major objections to closer political and economic relations between Ukraine and the West was widely understood to be a concern about NATO expansion, and the risk that would pose to Russia's military interests in the Crimean peninsula."[324] But, of course, why should we care what Putin or Russia fears, or believe is in their self-interest?

Meanwhile, there can be no doubt that many in Ukraine, particularly in the West which has strong anti-Russian sentiment, were angered by Yanukovych's vacillation on the EU deal and that this anger led to Yanukovych's undoing. What was bizarre, however, was how the US press reacted to Putin's offer, portraying it as somehow illegitimate for Putin to try to keep Ukraine within Russia's orbit by offering favorable terms.

Again, while it is obviously understandable that the EU was upset by this turn of events, why this was a major concern for the US simply does not stand to reason. It would be akin to Russia being upset about NAFTA—the three-way trade agreement between the US, Canada, and Mexico, which, by the way, has been devastating for Mexico in terms of destroying the livelihood of about two million Mexican small farmers and which helped make Mexico a failed state[325]—because it preferred that Mexico be more closely integrated with Brazil.

No one would care what Russia thought about such goings on in this Hemisphere anyway. Meanwhile, we seem to begrudge Russia for any assertion of self-interest even at its borders. It is as if Russia is to have no self-interest anywhere in the world, while the US should be able to assert its self-interest everywhere.

In any case, as we know, Yanukovych's backing away from the EU deal proved to be his undoing, with people taking to the streets and his being forced from office. Many of those protesting were regular folks who had legitimate concerns about the policies of Yanukovych—many of which were quite undemocratic and corrupt, no doubt—while some of those involved in the events of 2013–2014 were quite sinister.

Indeed, there were, and there are, those very closely aligned to the post-Yanukovych government of President Petro Poroshenko—who himself has asked the Ukraine Supreme Court to declare that the unseating of Yanukovych constituted an unconstitutional coup (most likely because he is afraid the same will happen to him)[326]—who are themselves violent, anti-democratic, and indeed neo-Nazi, and who are carrying out acts which accord with such a heinous philosophy.

And, there are certainly sectors of the US government who support these forces in Ukraine. These are undeniable facts, and yet it is rarely reported in the US press, and few seem concerned about it. From all appearances, the mainstream US media would prefer neo-Nazis running amok in Ukraine, and even taking charge, than having Ukraine integrated with Russia.

Max Blumenthal, writing at the time of the Euromaidan protests in February of 2014 which unseated Yanukovych, explained the facts on the ground:

> As the Euromaidan protests in the Ukrainian capital of Kiev culminated this week, displays of open fascism and neo-Nazi extremism became too glaring to ignore. Since demonstrators filled the downtown square to battle Ukrainian riot police and demand the ouster of the corruption-stained, pro-Russian President Viktor Yanukovych, it has been filled with far-right

streetfighting men pledging to defend their country's ethnic purity.

White supremacist banners and Confederate flags were draped inside Kiev's occupied City Hall, and demonstrators have hoisted Nazi SS and white power symbols over a toppled memorial to V.I. Lenin. After Yanukovych fled his palatial estate by helicopter, Euromaidan protesters destroyed a memorial to Ukrainians who died battling German occupation during World War II. *Sieg heil* salutes and the Nazi Wolfsangel symbol have become an increasingly common site in Maidan Square, and neo-Nazi forces have established "autonomous zones" in and around Kiev.[327]

As Blumenthal explains, "[o]ne of the 'Big Three' political parties behind the protests is the ultra-nationalist Svoboda, whose leader, Oleh Tyahnybok, has called for the liberation of his country from the 'Muscovite-Jewish mafia.'"[328] Despite Tyahnybok's openly neo-Nazi and anti-Semitic philosophy, the late Senator John McCain proudly rallied alongside him in Kiev.[329]

More disturbingly, as the recording of a call between Geoffrey Pyatt, the US ambassador to Ukraine, and Obama's assistant of State, Victoria Nuland, reveal, Nuland maneuvered behind to the scenes to make sure that the neo-Nazi Tyahnybok, while remaining officially "on the outside" of the new government, consulted with the US's choice for prime minister, Arseniy Yatsenyuk, "four times a week."[330]

As Nuland states in the same conversation, "I think Yats [Yatsenyuk] is the guy . . . ," as if it were for the US to handpick the new government.[331] And indeed, Nuland has admitted that, since 2004, the US has spent over $5 billion on promoting groups in Ukraine which would help align that country with the interests of the United States.[332] For his part, Barack Obama would later admit in an interview with CNN that he "had brokered a deal to transition power in Ukraine."[333] Again, the US may meddle wherever and whenever it wants, even half way around the world, while Russia must not assert its own interests even at its frontiers.

Even if it can be said that Putin overplayed his hand in trying to coax Yanukovych into rejecting the EU deal and accepting a deal with Russia, it is not at all surprising that Putin was nonetheless spooked by the events in Ukraine wherein neo-Nazis seemed to have a role in both the coup which deposed Yanukovych, and in the new government in Kiev. The fact that the US seemed to have a hand in these events, and to acquiesce in, if not outright encourage, the participation of ultra-nationalists in the Ukraine government was predictably disturbing to Putin as well.

More disturbingly, the US has had a hand in supporting Nazis in the Ukraine for a very long time. As an expert on this issue, Russ Bellant told *The Nation* magazine back in 2014[334] that "the key organization" in the 2014 Ukrainian coup was the Organization of Ukrainian Nationalists (OUN), which was founded in the 1920s, was actively in alliance with Nazi Germany as the "14th Waffen SS Division," and continues to defend its wartime role today. This group, which continues to wear the "SS" insignia on its uniforms, openly calls for the purging of Jews, Poles—and yes, of Russians as well—from Ukrainian society. Thousands of Ukrainian emigres associated with the OUN were resettled in the US after the war, and they have had great influence in the US, particularly within the Republican Party.

Bellant points out the inconvenient fact that the US has aggressively supported the OUN since WWII "through the intelligence agencies, initially military intelligence, later the CIA."

The OUN was also a key factor in the 2004 Orange Revolution—which the US was also behind—and Viktor Yuschenko, who was the prime minister of the Ukraine from 2005–2010, was closely aligned with them as they proceeded, among other things, to erect monuments to Nazi leaders throughout Ukraine. As Bellant explains, "[t]he United States was very aggressive in trying to keep the nationalists in power, but they lost the election" in 2010.

And so, the US pumped millions of dollars into Ukraine in the intervening period to help these nationalists return to power in the 2014 coup which precipitated the current crisis in Ukraine. The US has continued to provide military training to the ultra-nationalist forces post-coup—at first directly, and now, after Congress passed a law forbidding such training, as a consequence of their being so embedded in Kiev's regular forces.[335]

I share the view that of a number of commentators that, given the foregoing, Putin's response to the coup in the Ukraine was predictable, and even understandable. As John J. Mearsheimer, writing for Foreign Affairs, I think quite correctly writes:

> The United States and its European allies share most of the responsibility for the crisis. The taproot of the trouble is NATO enlargement, the central element of a larger strategy to move Ukraine out of Russia's orbit and integrate it into the West. At the same time, the EU's expansion eastward and the West's backing of the pro-democracy movement in Ukraine—beginning with the Orange Revolution in 2004—were critical elements, too. Since the mid-1990s, Russian leaders have adamantly opposed NATO enlargement, and in recent years, they have made it clear that they would not stand by while their strategically important neighbor turned into a Western bastion. For Putin, the illegal overthrow of Ukraine's democratically elected and pro-Russian president—which he rightly labeled a "coup"—was the final straw.[336]

Even if one does not go as far as putting the lion's share of the blame on the West for the Ukraine crisis, one at least has to understand why Putin and Russia would feel very threatened by these events. And frankly, the downplaying of the role of neo-Nazis in the current Ukrainian conflict is just baffling. For example, in an NPR piece in which Steve Inskeep interviewed the CEO of Voice of America, Inskeep mocked what he characterized as the "false flag" conspiracies of some who, apparently, deserve no voice in the Ukraine debate. The truth is, these alternative viewpoints have little to do with alarm over "false flags," but over Nazi flags. One would think this to be a worthy news item, but instead, it is dismissed out of hand.

Moreover, it would be unfair to say that it was only Putin and Russia which was disturbed by these events. The fact is that Ukrainians of Russian descent in the east of the country, particularly in the Donbass region, were also frightened by the nature of the new government, as were the residents of Crimea. And again, with good reason. It was not long before violent tensions began, and the blame for the violence that unfolded cannot be laid solely, or even primarily, at Putin's feet.

Again, former Reagan official, Paul Craig Roberts:

What has happened in Ukraine is the United States organized and financed a coup. And the coup occurred in Kiev, the capital. Either from intention or carelessness, the coup elements include ultra-right-wing nationalists whose roots go back to organizations that fought for Hitler in the Second World War against the Soviet Union. These elements destroyed Russian war memorials celebrating the liberation of the Ukraine from the Nazis by the Red Army and also celebrating Gen. Kutuzov's defeat of Napoleon's Grande Armée. So this spread a great deal of alarm in southern and eastern Ukraine, which are traditionally Russian provinces.

The other act which alarmed the "traditionally Russian provinces" was the vote in the Kiev parliament, almost immediately after the coup, to ban Russian as the second official language.

The result was that Pro-Russian separatists in Ukraine, without any prompting or support from Vladimir Putin—though that support would certainly come later—seized parts of the eastern Donetsk and Luhansk regions in March of 2014—very shortly after the coup—and declared their own "People's Republics," of course harkening back to the old Soviet Union.

In response, the new government in Kiev attacked the separatists in these regions in what they dubbed as "anti-terrorist" operations, and a brutal civil war has broken out. While the separatists have been vilified in the US media as pawns of Putin, this is just not the case. They are homegrown militants who want independence from the Kiev government which they view as illegitimate and fascist.

Of course, the US has been happy to support such separatists when it has served its own ends, as it did when it helped to break up the former Yugoslavia—even supporting, and indeed keeping on life support at a critical moment, the Kosovo Liberation Army (KLA) which was a designated terrorist organization[337]—and as it has done in Sudan when it helped South Sudan break away into its own independent state (that's going swimmingly by the way, with South Sudan now facing a potential genocide within its borders).[338]

Moreover, and quite ironically, while the US insisted on elections in Kosovo in regards to independence from Serbia as a condition to avoid the 1999 bombing—an insistence that helped derail possible peace—the US and EU were dead set against elections which the two Donbass regions called in November of 2014 to elect their own governments.[339] And, both the US and EU were critical of Russia's willingness to honor these elections. Of course, this goes to show again that it is the US which decides whether and when people can decide to declare their independence.

But even assuming that the people of the Donbass are not entitled to their own country, and even assuming that one is troubled that Putin's government in Moscow ended up following the lead of independent Russian militias in joining the fray in the Donbass, it is still fair to consider the forces on the other side that the Western governments and media are supporting against these peoples. While it is rare to hear this in the US mainstream press:

> Kiev's use of volunteer paramilitaries to stamp out the Russian-backed Donetsk and Luhansk "people's republics," proclaimed in eastern Ukraine in March, should send a shiver down Europe's spine. Recently formed battalions such as Donbas, Dnipro and Azov, with several thousand men under their command, are officially under the control of the interior ministry but their financing is murky, their training inadequate and their ideology often alarming.
>
> The Azov men use the neo-Nazi Wolfsangel (Wolf's Hook) symbol on their banner and members of the battalion are openly white supremacists, or anti-Semites.[340]

This same article from *The Telegraph* of London cites Mark Galeotti, an expert on Russian and Ukrainian security affairs at New York University, for the proposition that battalions like Azov are becoming "'magnets to attract violent fringe elements from across Ukraine and beyond,'" and "[t]he danger is that this is part of the building up of a toxic legacy for when the war ends."

How the proliferation of Nazis is not, by all appearances, of concern to the US press, while the concern about Putin has risen to pathological levels, is simply beyond me.

And, the fact is that the neo-Nazis are winning, with the civilian population of the Donbass taking a very bad beating as a result of the fighting, as well as from the siege being laid to that area by the government in Kiev.

Thus, as UNICEF has reported, *one million children in East Ukraine* are now in grave need of aid to survive.[341] UNICEF explains, not surprisingly given the horrible coverage of this situation, that **"[t]his is an invisible emergency—a crisis most of the world has forgotten."** (emphasis added). UNICEF further explains, "Children in eastern Ukraine have been living under the constant threat of unpredictable fighting and shelling for the past three years. Their schools have been destroyed, they have been forced from their homes and their access to basic commodities like heat and water has been cut off."

Not surprisingly, US support for the government in Ukraine has only been increasing under President Trump—a leader who seems quite comfortable with extremist right-wing groups. As Max Blumenthal wrote in early 2018, "[m]assive torchlit rallies pour out into the streets of Kiev on regular occasions, showcasing columns of Azov members rallying beneath the Nazi-inspired Wolfsangel banner that serves as the militia's symbol."[342] Blumenthal explains that Azov is a militia now incorporated into the Ukranian National Guard, and, despite its openly pro-Nazi ideology, including violent anti-Semitism, this militia has obtained heavy US weaponry transfers "right under the nose of the US State Department,' while "'US trainers and US volunteers' have been working closely with this battalion."

And so, the US seems to be right back where it was after WWII when it was willingly aligning with fascist forces in the name of fighting Communism in Europe and elsewhere. But of course, the Communist threat is now a thing of the fairly distant past, and obviously cannot explain US foreign policy in Ukraine or anywhere. However, there is something else which provides the explanation. As I quoted Stratfor's George Friedman at the outset of this chapter, the underlying goal of the US has been, for more than a century, to have dominion over the world, and its conduct of meddling and interfering abroad must be seen in the context of this aspiration. And while the US has claimed that it has a God-given right to such a dominant status because it is a beacon for peace and freedom around the globe, there is scant evidence of this.

CONCLUSION

IN HER LANDMARK PIECE IN *COMMENTARY*, Jean Kirkpatrick stated what many in the US accept as an article of faith: "[t]he United States is not in fact a racist, colonial power, it does not practice genocide, it does not threaten world peace with expansionist activities." It is this belief, so firmly held by many, which allows Americans to continue tolerating the US's serial interventionist policies abroad. The problem is that it is a false belief, and it is demonstrably so.

If one were paying attention, they would see the evidence of the US's interventionist and expansionist policies every day. The Central American children being ripped from their parents' arms, many to be abused by ICE officials, are evidence of the US's violent interventions in Guatemala, Honduras, and El Salvador. Mariee Juarez, a Guatemalan girl who was taken away from her mother at nineteen months old and who died in ICE custody, is just one such reminder.[343]

These immigrants come to our country to flee the violence our country has sewn in their homelands, only to be victimized again. Nicaragua has yet to send migrants *en masse* to our borders, the Sandinista leadership which the US has so opposed having succeeded in bringing some stability and prosperity to that country. But the US is now doing its damnedest to destroy this stability, hoping that a wall, perhaps, may be able to keep the resulting immigrants out.

When Haiti had its devastating earthquake in 2010 which killed tens of thousands, the US responded as it normally would to any crisis—it sent thousands of troops to invade the country. It did so upon the pretext of wanting to quell mass unrest that was happening in Haiti, when in fact there was no unrest at all.

As the *The Nation* later reported, "Washington deployed 22,000 troops to Haiti after the January 12, 2010, earthquake despite reports from the Haitian leadership, the US Embassy and the UN that no serious security threat existed, according to secret US diplomatic cables."[344]

Many Haitians believed that this militarized response to the crisis directly grew out of the centuries-old colonial, and indeed racist, attitude the US has had toward Haiti:

> "It is certain that one important reason for the US troop deployment to Haiti after the quake was to bar any revolutionary uprising that might have emerged due to the Haitian government's near collapse," said Haitian activist Ray Laforest, a member of the International Support Haiti Network. "Also the perception of Haitians in Washington, since the time of its 1915 occupation, is that they are savage, undisciplined and violent. In fact, the 2010 earthquake proved the opposite: Haitians came together in an exemplary display of heroism, resilience and solidarity. Washington's military response to the earthquake indicates how deeply it misunderstands, mistrusts and mistreats Haiti."[345]

Haitian refugees, also a reminder of the disastrous consequences of years of US intervention, are so reviled in the US that they were once listed by the CDC as one of the 4-Hs of the HIV epidemic: "homosexuals, heroin addicts, hemophiliacs and

Haitians."[346] As *PBS Frontline* explained, this racist stigma killed Haiti's crucial tourist industry, with tourism decreasing by 80 percent within a year of this designation.

The belief in our own superiority necessarily requires a belief in the inferiority of all others—some considered more inferior then others depending upon their skin tone—and both of these beliefs are critical to our ability to go from one disastrous intervention to the next without ever looking back, and without ever considering the consequences.

One country we have certainly never looked back to is the Democratic Republic of the Congo (DRC), but the effects of our policies continue to be felt today nonetheless, and new US policies—again based upon the notion that the US is somehow preeminent in the world—continue to destroy lives there. As Nick Turse wrote in August of 2018:

> What happened in the far east of the Democratic Republic of Congo earlier this year was a slaughter in silence. The wave of massacres was ignored by the world, and the humanitarian crisis that followed was amplified by international neglect. The Trump administration's "America First" agenda played no small part in this disaster; an abrupt change to US support for peacekeeping efforts in 2017 contributed to the constellation of catastrophes that enabled hundreds of machete-wielding militiamen to kill with impunity and cause immense suffering to hundreds of thousands of women, children and men.[347]

We will never know if the DRC might be a happy, stable country if we not only refrained from destroying Patrice Lumumba back in 1960, but if we even tried to help him bring happiness and stability to his people. Equally, we will never know what a country like Guatemala might have been if we had left Jacobo Arbenz to govern so many years ago. The same can be asked of Chile under Dr. Salvador Allende, the short, sweet-faced man with the famous horned-rimmed glasses, who the US decided to crush with extreme cruelty on September 11, 1973. What might have been if we had left him to carry out his socialist project in Chile?

Such questions can be asked about all of the interventions described in this book, and then some. And they must be asked if we are to find a different way to interact with the world—a way which does not seek to control or to dominate or, in so many cases, to destabilize and to destroy. If I have inspired people to at least start to ask such questions, then I have done my job.

ENDNOTES

1   "Executive Order on Imposing Certain Sanctions in the Event of Foreign Interference in a United States Election," September 12, 2018. Retrieved at: https://www.whitehouse.gov/presidential-actions /executive-order-imposing-certain-sanctions-event-foreign-interfer-ence-united-states-election/.

2   "Facebook and Twitter ban over 900 accounts in bid to tackle fake news," *Sky News* (Aug. 22, 2018). Retrieved at: https://news.sky .com/story/facebook-and-twitter-ban-over-900-accounts-in-bid-to -tackle-fake-news-11479022.

3   Josh Fox, "Here's How Your Unique Behavioral Psychological Profile Is Being Used to Manipulate You," *Seven Stories Press* (Sept. 13, 2018), as reprinted in *Alternet*. Retrieved at: https://www.alternet .org/how-do-we-know-whats-true.

4   *Id.*

5   Scott Shane, "Russia Isn't the Only One Meddling in Elections. We Do It, Too," *New York Times* (Feb. 17, 2018). Retrieved at: https: //www.nytimes.com/2018/02/17/sunday-review/russia-isnt-the-only -one-meddling-in-elections-we-do-it-too.html.

6   Dov H. Levin, "When the Great Power Gets a Vote: The Effects of Great Power Interventions on Election Results," *International Studies Quarterly*, Volume 60, Issue 2 (Feb. 13, 2016). Retrieved at: https://doi.org/10.1093/isq/sqv016.

7   Rich Whitney, "US Provides Military Assistance to 73 percent of World's Dictatorships," *Truthout* (September 23, 2017). Retrieved at: https://truthout.org/articles/us-provides-military-assistance-to-73-percent-of-world-s-dictatorships/.

8   Nobel Lecture: "Art, Truth & Politics," Harold Pinter, The Nobel Foundation 2005. Reprinted with Permission by the Nobel Committee. Retrieved at: https://www.nobelprize.org/prizes/literature/2005/pinter/25621-harold-pinter-nobel-lecture-2005/.

9   Ernesto Londoño and Nicholas Casey, "Trump Administration Discussed Coup Plans With Rebel Venezuelan Officers," *New York Times* (Sept. 9, 2018). Retrieved at: https://www.nytimes.com/2018/09/08/world/americas/donald-trump-venezuela-military-coup.html.

10   Eva Golinger, "The CIA Was Involved In the Coup Against Venezuela's Chavez," *Venezuela Analysis* (Nov. 22, 2004). Retrieved at: https://venezuelanalysis.com/analysis/800; Ed Vulliamy, "Venezuela Coup Linked to Team," *Guardian* (April 21, 2002). Retrieved at: https://www.theguardian.com/world/2002/apr/21/usa.venezuela.

11   *Id.*

12   David S. Heidler, Jeanne T. Heidler, "Manifest Destiny," Encyclopedia Britannica. Retrieved at: https://www.britannica.com/event/Manifest-Destiny.

13   *Id.*

14   *Id.*

15   Jeane J. Kirkpatrick, "Dictatorships and Double Standards," *Commentary* (Nov. 1, 1979). Retrieved at: https://www.commentarymagazine.com/articles/dictatorships-double-standards/.

16   Stephen G. Rabe, *The Killing Zone: The United States Wages Cold War in Latin America* (Oxford University Press, 2016), Second Edition, p. 5.

17   *Id.*

18   Matthew Wills, "The Ugly Origins of America's Involvement in The Philippines," *JSTOR Daily* (May 10, 2017). Retrieved at: https:

//daily.jstor.org/the-ugly-origins-of-americas-involvement-in-the
-philippines/.

19   *Id.*

20   British Frank, "The Philippines Genocide, 3 Million Filipinos
Killed," *Brits in The Philippines* (April 25, 2017). Retrieved at:
https://britsinthephilippines.top/philippines-genocide-3-million
-filipinos-killed/.

21   P.R. Lockhart, "Trump is ignoring one huge factor in the current
status of Haiti: US foreign policy," *Vox* (Jan. 12, 2018). Retrieved at:
https://www.vox.com/policy-and-politics/2018/1/12/16883224
/trump-shithole-foreign-policy-haiti.

22   *Id.*

23   Vanessa Buschschluter, "The long history of troubled ties between
the Haiti and the US," *BBC* (Jan. 16, 2010). Retrieved at: http://news
.bbc.co.uk/2/hi/americas/8460185.stm; see also, Kiki Makandal,
"100 Years of Imperialist Domination: The US Occupation of
Haiti (1915–34) and its current consequences," *Idées Nouvelles/Idées
Prolétarienes* (July 28, 2015). Retrieved at: http://koleksyon-inip
.org/100-years/.

24   Kiki Makandal, *id.*

25   Stephen G. Rabe, *id.* at ps. 1–8.

26   *Id.*

27   Smedley D. Butler, *War is a Racket: The Antiwar Classic by America's
Most Decorated Soldier.* Retrieved at: https://www.goodreads.com
/quotes/253269-i-spent-33-years-and-four-months-in-active-military.

28   Stephen G. Rabe, *id.* at 21.

29   Stephen G. Rabe, *id.* at p. 1.

30   *Id.* at p. 23–24.

31   *Id.*

32   Howard Zinn, *A People's History of The United States* (New York:
Harper & Row Publishers, 1980). Chapter 16. Retrieved at: https:
//web.viu.ca/davies/H323Vietnam/zinn.htm.

33 Office of the Historian, US State Department, "Milestones 1945–1952: The Truman Doctrine, 1947." Retrieved at: https://history.state.gov /milestones/1945–1952/truman-doctrine.

34 *Id.*

35 "The Greek Tragedy: Some Things not to forget, which the new Greek leaders have not," *The Anti-Empire Report*, William Blum, February 23, 2015.

36 *Id.*

37 Tim Weiner, "CIA Spent Millions to Support Japanese Right in 50s and 60s," *New York Times* (1994). Retrieved at: https://www.nytimes .com/1994/10/09/world/cia-spent-millions-to-support-japanese -right-in-50-s-and-60-s.html.

38 Stephen Gowans, *Patriots, Traitors and Empires: The Story of Korea's Fight for Freedom* (Baraka Books, 2018).

39 *Id.*

40 Tim Weiner, "F. Mark Wyatt, 86, C.I.A. Officer, Is Dead," *New York Times* (July 6, 2006). Retrieved at: https://www.nytimes.com/2006 /07/06/us/06wyatt.html.

41 Ishaan Tharoor, "The long history of the US interfering with elections elsewhere," *Washington Post* (Oct. 13, 2016). Retrieved at: https://www.washingtonpost.com/news/worldviews/wp/2016/10 /13/the-long-history-of-the-u-s-interfering-with-elections-else where/?noredirect=on&utm_term=.afc98b76b313.

42 Thomas Carothers, "Backing the Wrong Tyrant," *New York Times* (1994). Retrieved at: https://www.nytimes.com/1994/06/12/books /backing-the-wrong-tyrant.html.

43 William Blum, "A Brief History of US Interventions, 1945 to the Present," *Z Magazine* (June 1999). Retrieved at: http://www.thirdworld traveler.com/Blum/US_Interventions_WBlumZ.html.

44 Mynardo Macaraig, "Marcos: A US-Backed Dictator with Charisma," *Agence France-Presse* (Nov. 8, 2016). Retrieved at: https://news.abs -cbn.com/news/11/08/16/marcos-a-us-backed-dictator-with-charisma.

45 *Id.*

46   Belen Fernandez, "Paramilitarism and the assault on Democracy in Haiti," *Al Jazeera* (Oct. 4, 2012) (citing, Jeb Sprague, Paramilitarism and the assault on Democracy in Haiti (Monthly Review Press, 2012). Retrieved at: https://www.aljazeera.com/indepth/opinion/2012/09/201293072613719320.html.

47   *Id.*

48   *Id.*

49   Stephen Engelberg, Howard W. French, Tim Weiner "C.I.A. Formed Haitian Unit Later Tied to Narcotics Trade," *New York Times* (1993). Retrieved at: https://www.nytimes.com/1993/11/14/world/cia-formed-haitian-unit-later-tied-to-narcotics-trade.html.

50   Belen Fernandez, *id.*

51   *Id.*

52   Stephen Engelberg, "A Haitian leader of Paramilitaries was paid by C.I.A.," *New York Times* (1994). Retrieved at: https://www.nytimes.com/1994/10/08/world/a-haitian-leader-of-paramilitaries-was-paid-by-cia.html.

53   Maura R. O'Connor, "Subsidizing Starvation, How American tax dollars are keeping Arkansas rice growers fat on the farm and starving millions of Haitians," *Foreign Policy* (Jan. 11, 2013). Retrieved at: https://foreignpolicy.com/2013/01/11/subsidizing-starvation/.

54   *Id.*

55   Bill Quigley, "Why the US Owes Haiti Billions—The Briefest History," *Huffington Post* (May 25, 2001). Retrieved at: https://www.huffingtonpost.com/bill-quigley/why-the-us-owes-haiti-bil_b_426260.html.

56   Greg Guma, "U.S. Imperial Ways in Haiti. A History of Regime Change," *Global Research* (Jan. 30, 2017). Retrieved at: https://www.globalresearch.ca/u-s-imperial-ways-in-haiti-a-history-of-regime-change/5571770.

57   *Id.*; and Belen Fernandez, *id.*

58   Bill Quigley, *id.*

59   Belen Fernandez, *id.* (quoting, Greg Grandin).

60 P.R. Lockhart, *Id.*

61 Stephen F. Cohen, *Soviet Fates And Lost Alternatives* (Columbia University Press, 1993) at 154–155.

62 National Center for Biotechnology Information, US National Library of Medicine, Tamara Men, scientist, Paul Brennan, scientist, Paolo Boffetta, unit chief, and David Zaridze, director (Oct. 25, 2003). Retrieved at: https://www.ncbi.nlm.nih.gov/pmc/articles /PMC259165/.

63 "Meddling in Presidential Elections: Two Cases," Markar Melkonian at http://hetq.am/eng/news/74607/meddling-in-presidential-elections -two-cases.html, citing, "Boris Yeltsin," David Satter, *Wall Street Journal*, April 4, 2007 at https://hudson.org/research/4893-boris -yeltsin.

64 Congressional Research Service, Report 98–725, Stuart D. Goldman, Foreign Affairs and National Defense Division. Retrieved at: https://file.wikileaks.org/file/crs/98–725.pdf.

65 *Rescuing Boris*, Michael Kramer/Moscow, *Time*, July 15, 1996. http: //content.time.com/time/subscriber/article/0,33009,984833,00 .html.

66 Melkonian, *Ibid.*

67 F. William Engdahl, Manifest Destiny, Democracy as Cognitive Dissonance (mine.Books, 2018), p. 63.

68 Eleanor Randolph, "Americans Claim Role in Yeltsin Win," *LA Times* (July 9, 1996). Retrieved at: http://articles.latimes.com /1996-07-09/news/mn-22423_1_boris-yeltsin.

69 Engdahl, *id., citing*, Anne Williamson, Testimony Before the Committee on Banking and Financial Services of the US House of Representatives, Sept. 21, 1999.

70 Melkonian, *Ibid.*

71 *Id.*

72 *Id.* (citing, Simon Schuster, "Rewriting Russian History: Did Boris Yeltsin Steal the 1996 Presidential Election?" *Time*, Feb. 12, 2012.).

73   Alexander Kolesnichenko How October 1993 led to President Putin," *Russia Beyond The Headlines* (Oct. 3, 2013). Retrieved at: http://rbth.com/amp/500009.

74   *Id.*

75   *Id.*

76   Julie Makinen, "White House: China Should Account for Tiananmen Square Victims," *LA Times* (June 4, 2014). Retrieved at: http://www.latimes.com/world/asia/la-fg-tiananmen-white-house-china-victims-20140604-story.html. Of course, the White House never asked Yeltsin to account for the Duma massacre victims.

77   Cohen, *ibid.*

78   Helsinki Watch 1996 Human Rights Report on Russian Federation. Retrieved at: https://www.hrw.org/reports/1996/WR96/Helsinki-16.htm (Creative Commons License).

79   *Id.*

80   *Id.*

81   Harrison Samphir, "Paul Craig Roberts on Crimea, US Foreign Policy and the Transformation of Mainstream Media," *Truthout* (March 18, 2014). Retrieved at: http://www.truth-out.org/news/item/22542-paul-craig-roberts-on-crimea-us-foreign-policy-and-the-transformation-of-mainstream-media.

82   Cohen, *id.*

83   *Id.*

84   Kinzer, Stephen, *ibid.*

85   *Id.*

86   "April 16, 1953, Memo from Chief of Iran Branch, Near East and Africa Division (Waller) to the Chief of the Near East Africa Division, Directorate of Plans, Central Intelligence Agency (Roosevelt)," 2017 CIA Release, p.527. https://history.state.gov/historicaldocuments/frus1951-54Iran/d192.

87   Kinzer, Stephen, *ibid.*

88   2017 CIA Release, ps. 578–579, "Memorandum of Conversation," May 30, 1953. https://history.state.gov/historicaldocuments/frus1951-54Iran/d212.

89   *Id.*

90   2017 CIA Release, ps. 595–596, "Memorandum of Conversation,"
      June 19, 1953. https://history.state.gov/historicaldocuments/frus
      1951-54Iran/d220.

91   2017 CIA Release, p. 546, "Telegram From the Embassy in Iran
      to the Department of State," May 4, 1953. https://history.state.gov
      /historicaldocuments/frus1951-54Iran/d199.

92   2017 CIA Release, ps. 595–596, "Memorandum of Conversation,"
      June 19, 1953. https://history.state.gov/historicaldocuments/frus
      1951-54Iran/d220.

93   2017 CIA Release, ps. 567–568, "Memorandum From the Counselor
      of Embassy (Mattison) to the Ambassador of Iran (Henderson),
      May 19, 1953. https://history.state.gov/historicaldocuments/frus1951
      -54Iran/d206.

94   2017 CIA Release, p. 555, "Telegram From the Embassy in Iran to
      the Department of State," May 8, 1953. https://history.state.gov/
      historicaldocuments/frus1951-54Iran/d203.

95   2017 CIA Release, p. 612, "Despatch From the Embassy in Iran
      to the Department of State," July 1, 1953. https://history.state.gov
      /historicaldocuments/frus1951-54Iran/d233.

96   2017 CIA Release, "Memorandum From the Chief of the Near East
      and Africa Division, Directorate of Plans, Central Intelligence
      Agency (Roosevelt) to Mitchell, July 8, 1953. https://history.state.
      gov/historicaldocuments/frus1951-54Iran/d236.

97   2017 CIA Release, "Memorandum From the Acting Chief of the Near
      East and Africa Division, Directorate of Plans, Central Intelligence
      Agency 9[name not declassified]) to Mitchell," July 22, 1953.
      https://history.state.gov/historicaldocuments/frus1951-54Iran
      /d245.

98   2017 CIA Release, ps. 472–474, "Memorandum Prepared in the
      Directorate of Plans, Central Intelligence Agency," March 3, 1953.
      https://history.state.gov/historicaldocuments/frus1951-54Iran
      /d170.

99   2017 CIA Release, p. 536, "Memorandum From the Chief of the Iran Branch, Near East and Africa Division (Waller) to the Chief of the Near East and Africa Division, Directorate of Plans, Central Intelligence Agency (Roosevelt)," April 16, 1953. https://history.state.gov/historicaldocuments/frus1951-54Iran/d192.

100 2017 CIA Release, p. 503, "Progress Report to the National Security Council," March 20, 1953. https://history.state.gov/historical documents /frus1951-54Iran/d180.

101 Wilayto, Phil, *ibid.*

102 2017 CIA Release, p. 680, "Memorandum Prepared in the Office of National Estimates, Central Intelligence Agency," August 17, 1953. https://history.state.gov/historicaldocuments/frus1951-54Iran /d275.

103 2017 CIA Release, p. 664, "Telegram From the Embassy in Iran to the Department of State," August 16, 1953. https://history.state. gov/historicaldocuments/frus1951-54Iran/d262.

104 12017 CIA Release, ps. 685–686, "Telegram From the Embassy in Iran to the Department of State," August 18, 1953. https://history .state.gov/historicaldocuments/frus1951-54Iran/d280.

105 2017 CIA Release, p. 699, "Telegram From the Station in Iran to the Central Intelligence Agency," August 19, 1953. https://history .state.gov/historicaldocuments/frus1951-54Iran/d286.

106 2017 CIA Release, p. 701, "Telegram From the Station in Iran to the Central Intelligence Agency," August 20, 1953. https://history .state.gov/historicaldocuments/frus1951-54Iran/d289.

107 2017 CIA Release, p. 740, "Monthly Report Prepared in the Directorate of Plans, Central Intelligence Agency," August, 1953. https: //history.state.gov/historicaldocuments/frus1951-54Iran/d308.

108 2017 CIA Release, ps. 778–780, "Monthly Report Prepared in Directorate of Plans, Central Intelligence Agency," September, 1953. https://history.state.gov/historicaldocuments/frus1951-54Iran /d326.

109 2017 CIA Release, ps. 835–836, "Despatch From the Station in Iran to the Chief of the Near East and Africa Division, Directorate of Plans, Central Intelligence Agency (Roosevelt)," November 13, 1953. https://history.state.gov/historicaldocuments/frus1951-54Iran/d346.

110 2017 CIA Release, p. 927, "Editorial Note." https://history.state.gov/historicaldocuments/frus1951-54Iran/d372.

111 2017 CIA Release, p. 933, "National Intelligence Estimate," December 7, 1954. https://history.state.gov/historicaldocuments/frus1951-54Iran/d375.

112 2017 CIA Release, ps. 826–827, "Despatch From the Embassy in Iran to the Department of State," November 5, 1953. https://history.state.gov/historicaldocuments/frus1951-54Iran/d344.

113 Kinzer, Stephen, *ibid.*

114 2017 CIA Release, 950, Appendix, Summary of the Terms of the Oil Agreement between the International Oil Consortium and the Government of Iran, Signed 30 October 1954," https://history.state.gov/historicaldocuments/frus1951-54Iran/d375.

115 Kinzer, Steven, *ibid.*

116 Kinzer, Stephen, *ibid*; and Fisk, Robert, *ibid.*

117 Dean Henderson, *Big Oil & Their Bankers in The Persian Gulf: Four Horsemen, Eight Families & Their Global Intelligence, Narcotics & Terror Network 3rd Edition* (Create Space, 2010).

118 Jonathan C. Randal, "SAVAK Jails Stark Reminder of Shah's Rule," *Washington Post* (December 13, 1979).

119 Robert Fisk, *id.*

120 A.J. Langguth, "Torture's Teachers," *New York Times* (June 11, 1979).

121 Amnesty International Briefing: Iran, November 1, 1976. https://www.amnesty.org/download/Documents/204000/mde130011976en.pdf.

122 *Id.*

123 *Id.*

124   Robert Parry, "A CIA Hand in An American Coup?" *Consortium News* (August 26, 2013). Retrieved at: https://consortiumnews .com/2013/08/26/a-cia-hand-in-an-american-coup/.

125   Noam Chomsky, "1944–1989: The coup and US intervention in Guatemala," *What Uncle Sam Really Wants*. Retrieved at: https: //libcom.org/history/articles/guatemala-us-intervention.

126   *Id.*

127   Nicholas Cullather, "Operation PBSUCCESS: The United States and Guatemala, 1952–1954," Center for the Study of Intelligence, Central Intelligence Agency, Washington, D.C. 1994. Retrieved at: https://nsarchive2.gwu.edu/NSAEBB/NSAEBB4/docs/doc05.pdf.

128   Cullather, *id.*

129   David Talbot, *The Devil's Chessboard: Allen Dulles, the CIA, and the Rise of America's Secret Government* (Harper Perennial, 2015), p. 260.

130   Cullather, *id.*

131   Cullather, *id.*

132   Eduardo Galeano, *Open Veins of Latin America: Five Centuries of the Pillage of a Continent* (Monthly Review Press, 1977), p. 113.

133   Gerald Coby, *Thy Will Be Done: The Conquest of the Amazon: Nelson Rockefeller and Evangelism in the Age of Oil* (Open Road Media, 2017).

134   Ann Louise Bardach, "E. Howard Hunt's Final Confession, The Monstrous Spy Master Gloats Over His Crimes," *Slate* (Aug. 25, 2004). Retrieved at: http://www.slate.com/articles/news_and _politics/recycled/2007/01/e_howard_hunts_final_confession .html.

135   William Blum, "The Anti-Empire Report, #156," March 15, 2018. Retrieved at: https://williamblum.org/aer/read/156.

136   Amnesty International, Guatemala, A government program of polit- ical murder (Amnesty International Publications, 1981). Retrieved at: https://www.amnesty.org/download/Documents/200000/amr 340021981en.pdf.

137   Allan Nairn, "The CIA and Guatemala's Death Squads," *The Nation* (April 17, 1995). Retrieved at: https://libcom.org/library/cia -death-squads-allan-nairn.

138 Luke Moffett, "Guatemala's history of genocide hurts Mayan communities to this day," *The Conversation*, (June 18, 2018). Retrieved at: https://bit.ly/2wwOH8F.

139 Robert Perry, "How Reagan Promoted Genocide," *Consortium News* (Feb. 6, 2014). Retrieved at: https://consortiumnews.com/2014/02/06/how-reagan-promoted-genocide-2/.

140 Steven Kinzer, "Guatemalan Unions Watch Plant Feud," *New York Times* (July 10, 1984). Retrieved at: https://www.nytimes.com/1984/07/10/world/guatemala-unions-watch-plant-feud.html.

141 Moffett, *id.*

142 Parry, *id.*

143 *Id.*

144 Moffett, *id.*

145 "Guatemala: UN Calls for Action on Murders of Human Rights Activists," *Telesur* (Aug. 9, 2018). Retrieved at: https://www.telesurtv.net/english/news/Guatemala-UN-Assassinations-Murder-of-Human-Rights-Activists-20180809-0016.html.

146 Georges Nzongola-Ntalaja, "Patrice Lumumba: the most important assassination of the 20th century, The US-sponsored plot to kill Patrice Lumumba, the hero of Congolese independence, took place 50 years ago today," *The Guardian* (Jan. 17, 2011). Retrieved at: https://www.theguardian.com/global-development/poverty-matters/2011/jan/17/patrice-lumumba-50th-anniversary-assassination.

147 Adam Hochschild, *King Leopold's Ghost, A Story of Greed, Terror, and Heroism in Colonial Africa* (Mariner Books, 1998), p. 13.

148 Dr. Neil A. Frankel, "Maps of Africa," *The Atlantic Slave Trade and Slavery in America*. Retrieved at: http://www.slaverysite.com/Body/maps.htm.

149 Adam Hochschild, *id.*, p. 11.

150 *Id.* at ps. 65–66.

151 *Id.* at ps. 81–82.

152 *Id.* at 233.

153 *Id.* at 233–234.

154 *Id.* at ps. 278–279.

155 Ludo De Witte, *The Assassination of Lumumba* (Verso 2001), p. xv.

156 *Id.*

157 *Id.* at p. 6.

158 Stephen R. Weissman, "Congo-Kinshasa: New Evidence Shows US Role in Congo's Decision to Send Patrice Lumumba to His Death," *allAfrica* (August 1, 2010). Retrieved at: https://allafrica.com/stories/201008010004.html.

159 De Witte, *id.* at ps.20–22.

160 Office of the Historian, "The Congo, Decolonization, and The Cold War, 1960–1965," US Department of State. Retrieved at: https://history.state.gov/milestones/1961–1968/congo-decolonization.

161 De Witte, *id.* at ps. 7–13.

162 Office of the Historian, FOREIGN RELATIONS OF THE UNITED STATES, 1964–1968, VOLUME XXIII, CONGO, 1960–1968, US Department of State. Retrieved at: https://history.state.gov/historicaldocuments/frus1964-68v23/d1.

163 Weissman, *id.*

164 Maurice Carney, "Was Patrice Lumumba's assassination of the last century?", *TRTWORLD* (Aug. 6, 2018). Retrieved at: https://www.trtworld.com/opinion/was-patrice-lumumba-s-assassination-the-most-important-of-the-last-century—19397.

165 Office of the Historian, FOREIGN RELATIONS OF THE UNITED STATES, 1964–1968, VOLUME XXIII, CONGO, 1960–1968, US Department of State. Retrieved at: https://history.state.gov/historicaldocuments/frus1964-68v23/d1.

166 De Witte, *id.* at p. 17.

167 *Id.*

168 *Id.*

169 Madeleine G. Kalb, "The CIA And Lumumba," *New York Times Magazine* (Aug. 2, 1981). Retrieved at: https://www.nytimes.com/1981/08/02/magazine/the-cia-and-lumumba.html.

170 Office of the Historian, FOREIGN RELATIONS OF THE UNITED STATES, 1964–1968, VOLUME XXIII, CONGO,

1960–1968, US Department of State. Retrieved at: https://history.state
.gov/historicaldocuments/frus1964-68v23/d1.

171 Weissman, *id.*

172 *Id.*

173 *Id.*

174 Carney, *id.*

175 Hochschild, *id.*, p. 303.

176 Office of the Historian, "The Congo, Decolonization, and The
Cold War, 1960–1965," US Department of State. Retrieved at: https:
//history.state.gov/milestones/1961–1968/congo-decolonization.

177 "1994 Rwanda Pull-Out Driven by Clinton White House," The
National Security Archive (April 16, 2015). Retrieved at: http:
//nsarchive.gwu.edu/NSAEBB/NSAEBB511/.

178 Excerpt from "Crisis in The Congo." Retrieved at: https://www
.youtube.com/watch?v=G1gYQseoCpU.

179 See, *e.g.,* "What Really Happened in Rwanda," BBC (2014).
Retrieved at: https://vimeo.com/107867605.

180 "The Clinton Legacy: Uplifting Rhetoric, Grim Realities" William
D. Hartung and Dena Montague, *World Policy Institute* (March 22,
2001). Retrieved at: http://www.worldpolicy.org/projects/arms
/reports/update032201.htm.

181 "Trump and the Contradictions," *The African Communist*, Issue 194,
February 2017.

182 The World Policy Institute, *id.*

183 *Id.*

184 "American Companies Exploit The Congo," *Project Censored* (Aug.
29, 2010). Retrieved at: http://projectcensored.org/19-american
-companies-exploit-the-congo/.

185 The World Policy Institute, *id.*

186 Richard C. Morais, "Friends in High Places," *Forbes* (Aug. 10, 1998).
Retrieved at: https://www.forbes.com/global/1998/0810/0109038a
.html.

187   UN Security Council Report (Oct. 16, 2002). Retrieved at: https://documents-dds-ny.un.org/doc/UNDOC/GEN/N02/621/79/PDF/N0262179.pdf?OpenElement.

188   *See*, *Crisis In The Congo*, and Gregory Stanton's remarks therein about Clinton's military support for the invasion of the Congo: https://www.youtube.com/watch?v=vLV9szEu9Ag; *See also*, Herman & Peterson, The Politics of Genocide (Monthly Review Press 2010).

189   "The World Capital of Killing," Nicholas Kristoff, *New York Times* (Feb. 6, 2010). Retrieved at: http://www.nytimes.com/2010/02/07/opinion/07kristof.html. *See also*, UN Mapping Report of the Conflict in the DRC, 1993–2003 (August 2010). Retrieved at: http://friendsofthecongo.org/pdf/mapping_report_en.pdf.

190   "Jerry Kuzmarov, "Black Lives Matter, But Not for Clinton," *Huffington Post* (April 22, 2016). Retrieved at: http://www.huffingtonpost.com/jeremy-kuzmarov/black-african-lives-matte_b_9763346.html.

191   Chomsky, Noam & Herman, Edward S., *The Washington Connection and Third World Fascism*, Haymarket Books (Chicago, 2014).

192   "1964: Brasil & CIA," *CounterSpy*, April-May, 1979, pp. 4–23, reprinted in *Brasil Wire* (March 13, 2016). Retrieved at: http://www.brasilwire.com/1964-brasil-cia/.

193   *Id.*

194   *Id.*

195   *Id.*

196   Jan Knippers Black, "The US and Brazil: On Reaping What You Sow," *NACLA* (March 6, 2015).

197   *CounterSpy, id.*

198   *Id.*

199   Anthony W. Pereira, "The US Role in the 1964 Coup in Brazil: A Reassessment," *Bulletin of Latin American Research—Wiley Online Library*. Retrieved at: https://onlinelibrary.wiley.com/doi/full/10.1111/blar.12518.

200   *Id.*

201 Jan Knippers Black, *id.*

202 Department of State briefing on "The Esquadrão da Morte (Death Squad)," June 8, 1971, Retrieved at: http://cnv.memoriasreveladas. gov.br/images/pdf/docs/Doc11_53384-6-002.pdf.

203 Memorandum of Conversation, Re: "Dominican Involvement in Terror," December 10, 1969. Retrieved at: http://cnv.memorias reveladas.gov.br/images/pdf/docs/Doc04_53384-4-001.pdf.

204 Memorandum of Conversation, Re: "Church-State Relations," March 6, 1972. Retrieved at: http://cnv.memoriasreveladas.gov.br /images/pdf/docs/Doc14_53384-6-005.pdf.

205 Message Text, From US Embassy in Brasilia to US Department of State, Re: "Dom Helder Camara Condemns Obsession With National Security And Defends Human Rights," Dec. 1977. Retrieved at: http://cnv.memoriasreveladas.gov.br/images/pdf/docs /Doc41_CFPF.1977BRASILIA10229.pdf.

206 "On Religion and Politics," Noam Chomsky interviewed by Amina Chaudary, *Islamica Magazine*, Issue 19, April–May 2007. Retrieved at: https://chomsky.info/200704___/.

207 Ted Snider, "A US Hand in Brazil's Coup?", *Consortium News* (June 1, 2016). Retrieved at: https://consortiumnews.com/2016/06 /01/a-us-hand-in-brazils-coup/.

208 Brasil Wire Editors, "Hidden History: The US 'War on Corruption' in Brazil," *Truthdig* (Feb. 4, 2018). Retrieved at: https://www .truthdig.com/articles/hidden-history-u-s-war-corruption-brazil/.

209 "Brazil's ex-president Lula imprisoned to keep him out of the election," Professor David Treece, et al., *The Guardian*, June 8, 2018. Retrieved at: https://www.theguardian.com/world/2018/jun/08 /brazils-ex-president-lula-imprisoned-to-keep-him-out-of-the-election -letters.

210 "UN: Brazil's jailed ex-president Lula can't be disqualified from election," *Agence France-Presse*, August 17, 2018. Retrieved at: https://www.theguardian.com/world/2018/aug/17/un-brazils-jailed -leader-lula-cant-be-disqualified-from-election.

211   Jan Knippers Black, *id.*

212   David Miranda, "The real reason Dilma Rousseff's enemies want her impeached," *The Guardian* (April 21, 2016). Retrieved at: https://goo.gl/ZZccDm.

213   *Truthdig, id.*

214   Jill Langolis, "It's been a deadly season for environmental activists and land defenders in Brazil," *LA Times* (August 1, 2018). Retrieved at: http://www.latimes.com/world/la-fg-brazil-environmentalists-killed-20180801-story.html.

215   Ernesto Londoño and Manuela Andreoni, "Brazil's Military Strides Into Politics, by the Ballot or by Force," *New York Times* (July 21, 2018). Retrieved at: https://www.nytimes.com/2018/07/21/world/americas/brazils-election-military.html.

216   Flávia Milhorance, "Brazil: murder of indigenous leader highlights threat to way of life," *The Guardian* (Aug. 16, 2018). Retrieved at: https://www.theguardian.com/environment/2018/aug/16/brazil-jorginho-guajajara-amazon-indigenous-leader.

217   Ho Chi Minh letter to US Secretary of State, Oct. 18, 1945. Retrieved at: http://www.historyisaweapon.com/defcon2/hochiminh/.

218   Fox Butterfield, "Pentagon Papers: Eisenhower Decisions Undercut the Geneva Accords, Study Says," *New York Times* (July 5, 1971). Retrieved at: https://www.nytimes.com/1971/07/05/archives/pentagon-papers-eisenhower-decisions-undercut-the-geneva-accords.html.

219   *Id.*

220   *Id.*

221   Nick Turse, *Kill Anything That Moves: The Real American War in Vietnam* (Henry Holt & Company, 2013), ps. 2–3.

222   *Id.*, p. 1.

223   *Id.*, p. 60.

224   Chomsky & Herman, *id.*, p. 355.

225   John A. Farrell, "When a Candidate Conspired With a Foreign Power to Win an Election," *Politico* (Aug. 6, 2017). Retrieved at: https://www.politico.com/magazine/story/2017/08/06/nixon

-vietnam-candidate-conspired-with-foreign-power-win-election
-215461.

226 Farrell, *id.*

227 Robert Parry, "The Heinous Crime Behind Watergate," *Consortium News* (Aug. 9, 2014). Retrieved at: https://consortiumnews.com /2014/08/09/the-heinous-crime-behind-watergate/.

228 Turse, *id.,* ps. 208–212.

229 *Id.*, p. 212.

230 *Id.*, ps. 190–191.

231 Robert Parry, *id.*

232 *Id.*

233 Chomsky & Herman, *id.*, 109–110.

234 *Id.*

235 "Who Supported The Khmer Rouge," Gregory Elich, Counterpunch (Oct. 16, 2014). Retrieved at: http://www.counterpunch .org/2014/10/16/who-supported-the-khmer-rouge/.

236 Hobsbawm, *Ibid* at p. xv.

237 *Id.*

238 Robert Parry, *Id.*

239 William Blum, *Killing Hope, US Interventions Since World War II* (Zed Books, 2014), p. 383.

240 Monte Reel and J.Y. Smith, "A Chilean Dictator's Dark Legacy," *Washington Post* (Dec. 11, 2006). Retrieved at: http://www.washing tonpost.com/wp-dyn/content/article/2006/12/10/AR2006121 000302.html.

241 Peter Kornbluh, *The Pinochet File: A Declassified Dossier on Atrocity and Accountability* (The New Press 2004), p. 4.

242 *Id.* at p. 5.

243 "CIA Activities in Chile," Sept. 18, 2000. Retrieved at: https://www .cia.gov/library/reports/general-reports-1/chile/.

244 Kornbluh, *id.* at ps. 1–2.

245 *Id.* at p. 14.

246 *Id. at p. 1.*

247 "CIA Activities in Chile," *id.*

248 *Id.*; and Kornbluh, *id.* at ps. 22–29.

249 Ishaan Thorer, "The Long History of US Interfering with Elections Elsewhere," *Washington Post* (Oct. 13, 2016). Retrieved at: https://www.washingtonpost.com/news/worldviews/wp/2016/10/13/the-long-history-of-the-u-s-interfering-with-elections-elsewhere/?noredirect=on&utm_term=.afc98b76b313.

250 "Pinochet's Chile," *Washington Post*. Retrieved at: http://www.washingtonpost.com/wp-srv/inatl/longterm/pinochet/overview.htm.

251 Juan Garces & Peter Kornbluh,"The Pinochet File: How US Politicians, Bankers and Corporations Aided Chilean Coup, Dictatorship," *Democracy Now!* (Sept. 10, 2013). Retrieved at: http://m.democracynow.org/web_exclusives/1883.

252 Zoltan Zigedy, "Remembering Chile," *ZZ's Blog* (Sept. 7, 2018). Retrieved at: http://zzs-blg.blogspot.com/ Citing, James Petras and Morris Morley, The United States and Chile: Imperialism and the Overthrow of the Allende Government (Monthly Review Press, 1975).

253 Buloet Gokay, "In Saudi Arabia's quest to debilitate the Iranian economy, they destroyed Venezuela," *Independent* (Aug. 9, 2017). Retrieved at: https://www.independent.co.uk/voices/venezuela-saudi-arabia-oil-prices-iran-price-war-inflation-destabilisation-a7883846.html.

254 Shashank Bengali and Ramin Mostaghim, "The return of US sanctionsis is expected to sow misery in Iran," *LA Times* (May 29, 2018). Retrieved at: http://www.latimes.com/world/middleeast/la-fg-iran-economy-2018-story.html#.

255 Buloet Gokay, id.

256 Janine Jackson and Joe Emersberger, "These Are Sanctions Directly Aimed at the Civilian Population," *FAIR* (May 1, 2018). Retrieved at: https://fair.org/home/these-are-sanctions-directly-aimed-at-the-civilian-population/.

257 *Id.*

258 Mark Weisbrot,"Behind The Scenes in Venezuela," *US News & World Report* (March 3, 2018). Retrieved at: https://www.usnews .com/opinion/world-report/articles/2018-03-03/new-evidence-the -trump-administration-is-meddling-in-venezuelas-elections.

259 Weisbrot, *id.*

260 *Id.*

261 "CIA Activities in Chile," *id.*

262 Galeano, *id.* at ps. 270–271.

263 Vltchek, Andre. *Western Terror From Potosi to Baghdad*, (Mainstay Press, 2006).

264 "Victor Jara killing: Nine Chilean ex-soldiers sentenced," *BBC* (July 4, 2018). Retrieved at: https://www.bbc.com/news/world -latin-america-44709924.

265 Adam Feinstein, "Pablo Neruda: experts say official cause of death 'does not reflect reality'," *The Guardian* (Oct. 23, 2017). Retrieved at: https://www.theguardian.com/books/2017/oct/23/pablo-neruda -experts-say-official-cause-of-death-does-not-reflect-reality.

266 *Id.*

267 Kornbluh, *id.* at p. 13.

268 "Thousands of Chilean children who were adopted outside of the country during Augusto Pinochet's dictatorship are suspected to have been stolen," *Telesur* (Sept. 8, 2018). Retrieved at: https://www .facebook.com/teleSUREnglish/videos/261375831249673/.

269 "Victims of Operation Condor By Country," Ben Norton (May 28, 2015). Retrieved at: http://bennorton.com/victims-of-operation -condor-by-country/.

270 Joseph Nevins, "How US policy in Honduras set the state for today's mass migration," *The Conversation* (Oct. 31, 2016) (citing, Walter LeFeber, "Inevitable Revolutions: The United States in Central America"). Retrieved at: https://theconversation.com/how-us -policy-in-honduras-set-the-stage-for-todays-mass-migration-65935.

271 *Id.*

272   *Id.*

273   *Id.*

274   "Honduran coup shows business elite still in charge," Alexandra Olson. Associated Press (Aug. 2009). Retrieved at: http://www.newsday .com/honduran-coup-shows-business-elite-still-in-charge-1.1353372.

275   James Hodge and Linda Cooper, "U.S. Continues To Train Honduras Troops," *National Catholic Reporter* (July 14, 2009). Retrieved at: https://www.ncronline.org/news/global/us-continues -train-honduran-soldiers.

276   Jake Johnston, "How Pentagon Officials May Have Encouraged A 2009 Coup in Honduras," *The Intercept* (Aug. 29, 2017). Retrieved at:https://theintercept.com/2017/08/29/honduras-coup-us-defense -departmetnt-center-hemispheric-defense-studies-chds/.

277   *Id.*

278   "Testimony that US military really was involved in the 2009 Honduras coup: Statement of Martin Edwin Andersen to Department of Defense Inspector General Glenn Fine, on the Hands-On Role of Senior CHDS/ US Southern Command Staff in the 2009 Honduran Coup," May 23, 2016, Retrieved at: https://www .facebook.com/crossbordernetwork/posts/testimony-that-us-military -really-was-involved-in-the-2009-honduras-coupstatemen /10153842910279440/.

279   Mark Taliano "What Happens When Empire Intervenes in the Affairs of Other Countries," *Huffington Post* (Dec. 19, 2014). Retrieved at: http://www.huffingtonpost.ca/mark-taliano/canada -foreign-affairs_b_6011844.html.

280   Dan Beeton, "Investigation Reveals New Details of US Role in 2009 Honduras Military Coup," *CEPR online*, Retrieved at http: //cepr.net/press-center/press-releases/investigation-reveals-new -details-of-us-role-in-2009-honduras-military-coup.

281   Jake Johnson, *id.*

282   *Id.*

283   Roque Planas, "Hillary Clinton's Response To Honduran Coup Was Scrubbed From Her Paperback Memoirs," *Huffington Post*

(March 12, 2016). Retrieved at: http://www.huffingtonpost.com /entry/hillary-clinton-honduras-coup-memoirs_us_56e34161e4b0 b25c91820a08.

284 Jake Johnson, *id.*

285 Robert Naiman, "Wikileaks Honduras: State Dept. Busted on Support of Coup," *Huffington Post* (Nov. 29, 2010). Retrieved at: https://www.huffingtonpost.com/robert-naiman/wikileaks -honduras-state_b_789282.html.

286 Jake Johnson, *id.*

287 Lee Fang, "During Honduras Crisis, Clinton Suggested Back Channel With Lobbyist Lanny Davis," *The Intercept* (July 6, 2015). Retrieved at: https://theintercept.com/2015/07/06/clinton -honduras-coup/.

288 Dana Frank, "In Honduras, A Mess Made in America," *New York Times* (Jan. 27, 2012). Retrieved at: http://www.nytimes .com/2012/01/27/opinion/in-honduras-a-mess-helped-by-the-us .html.

289 "Before Her Assassination, Berta Cáceres Singled Out Hillary Clinton for Backing Honduran Coup," *DemocracyNow*! (March 11, 2016). Retrieved at: https://www.democracynow.org/2016/3/11 /before_her_assassination_berta_caceres_singled.

290 Jake Johnson, *Id.*

291 Nina Lakhani, "Berta Cáceres court papers show murder suspects' links to US-trained elite troops," *The Guardian* (Feb. 28, 2017). Retrieved at: https://www.theguardian.com/world/2017/feb/28 /berta-caceres-honduras-military-intelligence-us-trained-special -forces.

292 David Vine, *Base Nation: How US Military Bases Abroad Harm America and The World* (Metropolitan Books, 2015).

293 Democracy Now, *Ibid.*

294 Corey Kane, "Honduras: the most deadly place for journalists in the Americas," *Latin Correspondent* (Nov. 5, 2015). Retrieved at: http://latincorrespondent.com/2015/11/honduras-the-most-deadly -place-for-journalists-in-the-americas/#R5AuAP8me7A6WdAG.97.

295	Anna-Catherine Brigida, "Garifunas Flee Discrimination and Land Grabs In Record Numbers," *Telesur* (Feb. 23, 2017). Retrieved at: http://www.telesurtv.net/english/news/Garifuna-Flee-Discrimination -and-Land-Grabs-in-Record-Numbers-20170223-0002.html. *See also* the piece that I wrote on the same subject shortly after the coup: "Honduran Coup Government Continues Attack on the Poor with Plan to Seize Indigenous Hospital," *Huffington Post*. Retrieved at: http://www.huffingtonpost.com/dan-kovalik/honduran-coup -government_b_254033.html.

296	Doyle McManus, "Rights Groups Accuse Contras: Atrocities in Nicaragua Against Civilians Charged," *Los Angeles Times* (March 8, 1985).

297	Robert Parry, "Contras, Dirty Money and CIA," *Consortium News* (Dec. 19, 2013). Retrieved at: https://consortiumnews.com /2013/12/19/contras-dirty-money-and-cia/.

298	"The Iran-Contra Affair," *PBS*. Retrieved at: https://www.pbs.org /wgbh/americanexperience/features/reagan-iran/.

299	Prof. Ricardo Perez, "Cimientos de Democracia" (June 25, 2018). Retrieved at: http://www.redvolucion.net/2018/06/25/cimientos-de -la-democracia/.

300	Charles Litkey, et al., "U.S. Waged 'Low-Intensity' Warfare in Nicaragua," Dec. 1, 1989. Retrieved at: http://www.brianwillson .com/u-s-waged-low-intensity-warfare-in-nicaragua/.

301	S. Brian Willson, "How the US Purchased the 1990 Nicaraguan Elections," July 1, 1990. Retrieved at: http://www.brianwillson .com/how-the-u-s-purchased-the-1990-nicaragua-elections/.

302	Prof. Ricardo Perez, *id.*

303	Paul Baizerman, "The Nicaraguan Elections: US Government Promotes Fear and Divisiveness to Ensure Right-wing Victory," US International Election Observation Delegation. Retrieved at: https://www.yachana.org/reports/nica2001/baizerman.html.

304	William Blum, "The Anti-Empire Report, #156," March 15, 2018. Retrieved at: https://williamblum.org/aer/read/156.

305	*Id.*

306 *Id.*

307 Luca di Fabio, "Economic Growth In Nicaragua Has Helped Reduce Poverty," *The Borgen Project* (April 2018). Retrieved at: https://borgen project.org/economic-growth-in-nicaragua-helped-reduce-poverty/.

308 CELAC, "Primavera democrática en Nicaragua ¿anticipo del verano . . . o el invierno?", May 12, 2018. Retrieved at: http://www .celag.org/primavera-democratica-en-nicaragua-anticipo-del-verano -o-el-invierno/.

309 Prensa Latina, "Nicaraguan President Daniel Ortega at 80% Approval Rating," *Telesur* (Oct. 19, 2017). Retrieved at: https://www .telesurtv.net/english/news/Nicaraguan-President-Daniel -Ortega-at-80-Aproval-Rating-Poll-20171019-0008.html.

310 Corporación Latinobarómetro, Informe 2017. Retrieved at: https: //t.co/lqTEHMGmki.

311 Jorge Capelán and Stephen Sefto, "The left over Nicaragua: Between Pride and Ignorance," *Tortilla Con Sal* (May 16, 2018). Retrieved at: http://www.tortillaconsal.com/tortilla/node/2807.

312 John Perry, "After 2 Months of Unrest, Nicaragua is at a Fateful Crossroads," *The Nation* (June 22, 2018). Retrieved at: https://www.thenation.com/article/two-months-unrest-nicaragua -fateful-crossroad/.

313 Steve Sweeney, "Right-wing Militias committing "acts of terrorism" in an attempt to destabilize Nicaragua, Police Say," *Morning Star* (June 11, 2018). Retrieved at: https://www.morningstaronline .co.uk/article/f-lead-nicaraguan-acts-terrorism.

314 Max Blumenthal, "US Gov. Meddling Machine Boasts of 'Laying the Groundwork for Insurrection' in Nicaragua," *Grayzone Project* (2018). Retrieved at: https://grayzoneproject.com/2018/06/19/ned -nicaragua-protests-us-government/.

315 CELAG, *id.*

316 Elena Chernenko & Alexander Gubuev, "Stratfor Chief's 'Most Blatant Coup in History," *Kommersant* (Jan. 20, 2015). Retrieved at: https://russia-insider.com/en/politics/stratfor-chiefs-most-blatant -coup-history-interview-translated-full/ri2561.

317 Shaun Walker, "Vladimir Putin offers Ukraine financial incentives to stick with Russia," *The Guardian* (Dec. 18, 2013). Retrieved at: https://www.theguardian.com/world/2013/dec/17/ukraine-russia -leaders-talks-kremlin-loan-deal.

318 *Id.*

319 "Putin victorious as Ukraine postpones 'trade suicide', halts talks with EU," *RT News* (Nov. 24, 2013). Retrieved at: https://www .rt.com/business/ukraine-eu-deal-suspended-088/.

320 *Id.*

321 "Ukraine Blames I.M.F. for Halt to Agreements With Europe," David M. Herszenhorn, *New York Times* (Nov. 22, 2013). Retrieved at: http://www.nytimes.com/2013/11/23/world/europe /ukraine-blames-imf-for-collapse-of-accord-with-european-union .html.

322 Stephen F. Cohen interview with author, June 2015.

323 "Joint statement of the NATO-Ukraine Commission" (December 2014). Retrieved at: http://www.nato.int/cps/en/natohq/official _texts_115474.htm.

324 Andrew Higgins and David M. Herszenhorn, "Defying Russia, Ukraine Signs EU Trade Pact," *New York Times* (June 27, 2014). Retrieved at: https://www.nytimes.com/2014/06/28/world/europe /ukraine-signs-trade-agreement-with-european-union.html?_r=0.

325 Laura Carlsen, "Under Nafta, Mexico Suffered, and the United States Felt Its Pain," *New York Times* (Nov. 14, 2013). Retrieved at: http://www.nytimes.com/roomfordebate/2013/11/24/what-weve -learned-from-nafta/under-nafta-mexico-suffered-and-the-united -states-felt-its-pain.

326 Eric Zuesse, "Ukraine's Pres. Poroshenko Says Overthrow of Yanukovych Was a Coup," *Washington Blog* (June 22, 2015). Retrieved at: http://www.washingtonsblog.com/2015/06/ukraines-pres -poroshenko-says-overthrow-of-yanukovych-was-a-coup.html.

327 Max Blumenthal, "Is The US Backing Neo-Nazis in The Ukraine," *Salon* (Feb. 25, 2014). Retrieved at: http://www.salon.com/2014 /02/25/is_the_us_backing_neo_nazis_in_ukraine_partner/.

328 *Id.*

329 *Id.*

330 *Id.*

331 "Ukraine crisis: Transcript of leaked Nuland-Pyatt call," Transcript w/analysis by Jonathan Marcus, BBC (Feb. 7, 2014). Retrieved at: http://www.bbc.com/news/world-europe-26079957.

332 Paul Craig Roberts, *id.*

333 "Pres Obama on Fareed Zakaria GPS," CNN (Feb. 1, 2015). Retrieved at: http://cnnpressroom.blogs.cnn.com/2015/02/01/pres -obama-on-fareed-zakaria-gps-cnn-exclusive/.

334 Paul H. Rosenberg and Russ Bellant, "Seven Decades of Nazi Collaboration: America's Dirty Little Ukraine Secret," *The Nation* (March 28, 2014). Retrieved at: https://www.thenation.com/article /seven-decades-nazi-collaboration-americas-dirty-little-ukraine -secret/.

335 Will Cathcart and Joseph Epstein, "Is America Training Neo-Nazis in The Ukraine," *The Daily Beast* (July 4, 2015). Retrieved at: http: //www.thedailybeast.com/articles/2015/07/04/is-the-u-s-training -neo-nazis-in-ukraine.html.

336 Mearsheimer, *id.*

337 Dana Priest and Peter Finn, "NATO Gives Air Support to KLA Forces," *Washington Post* (June 2, 1999). Retrieved at: http://www .washingtonpost.com/wp-srv/inatl/longterm/balkans/stories/military 060299.htm.

338 Princeton Lyman and Nancy Lindborg, "We're ignoring a possible genocide in South Sudan," CNN (Dec. 15, 2016). Retrieved at: http://www.cnn.com/2016/12/15/opinions/south-sudan-genocide -looming/.

339 "Why are Ukraine separatist elections controversial?" *BBC News* (Nov. 1, 2014). Retrieved at: http://www.bbc.com/news/world-europe -29831028.

340 Tom Parfitt, "Ukraine crisis: the neo-Nazi brigade fighting pro-Russian separatists," *The Telegraph* (Aug. 11, 2014). Retrieved at: http:

//www.telegraph.co.uk/news/worldnews/europe/ukraine
/11025137/Ukraine-crisis-the-neo-Nazi-brigade-fighting-pro-Russian
-separatists.html.

341   "One million Ukrainian children now need aid as number doubles
over past year—UNICEF," UN News Centre (Feb. 17, 2017).
Retrieved at: http://www.un.org/apps/news/story.asp?NewsID=56193
#.WLbuTdIrLcv.

342   Max Blumenthal, "The US is Arming and Assisting Neo-Nazis in
Ukraine, While Congress Debate Prohibition," *Real News Network*
(Jan. 19, 2018).

343   Gina Martinez, "A Mother Says Her 19-month Daughter Died
After Being Held by ICE, Now She is suing for Millions,"
Time (Aug. 29, 2018). Retrieved at: http://time.com/5381834
/toddler-dies-after-leaving-texas-detention-center/.

344   Ansel Herz, "Wikileaks Cables: The Earthquake Files," *The Nation*
(June 15, 2011). Retrieved at: https://www.thenation.com/article
/wikileaks-haiti-earthquake-cables/.

345   *Id.*

346   "Haiti, The High Price of Stigma," *PBS Frontline* (June 19, 2006).
Retrieved   at: https://www.pbs.org/wgbh/pages/frontline/aids
/countries/ht.html.

347   Nick Turse, "A Slaughter in Silence," *Vice News* (Aug. 1, 2018).
Retrieved at: https://news.vice.com/en_us/article/7xq45a/a-slaughter
-in-silence-democratic-republic-of-the-congo.